# HIGH WYCOMBE IN 50 BUILDINGS

EDDIE BRAZIL

AMBERLEY

*For Sue and Bex*

First published 2021

Amberley Publishing, The Hill, Stroud
Gloucestershire GL5 4EP

www.amberley-books.com



British Library Cataloguing in Publication Data.
A catalogue record for this book is available from the British Library.

ISBN 978 1 4456 9762 8 (print)
ISBN 978 1 4456 9763 5 (ebook)

Typesetting by SJmagic DESIGN SERVICES, India.
Printed in Great Britain.

# Contents

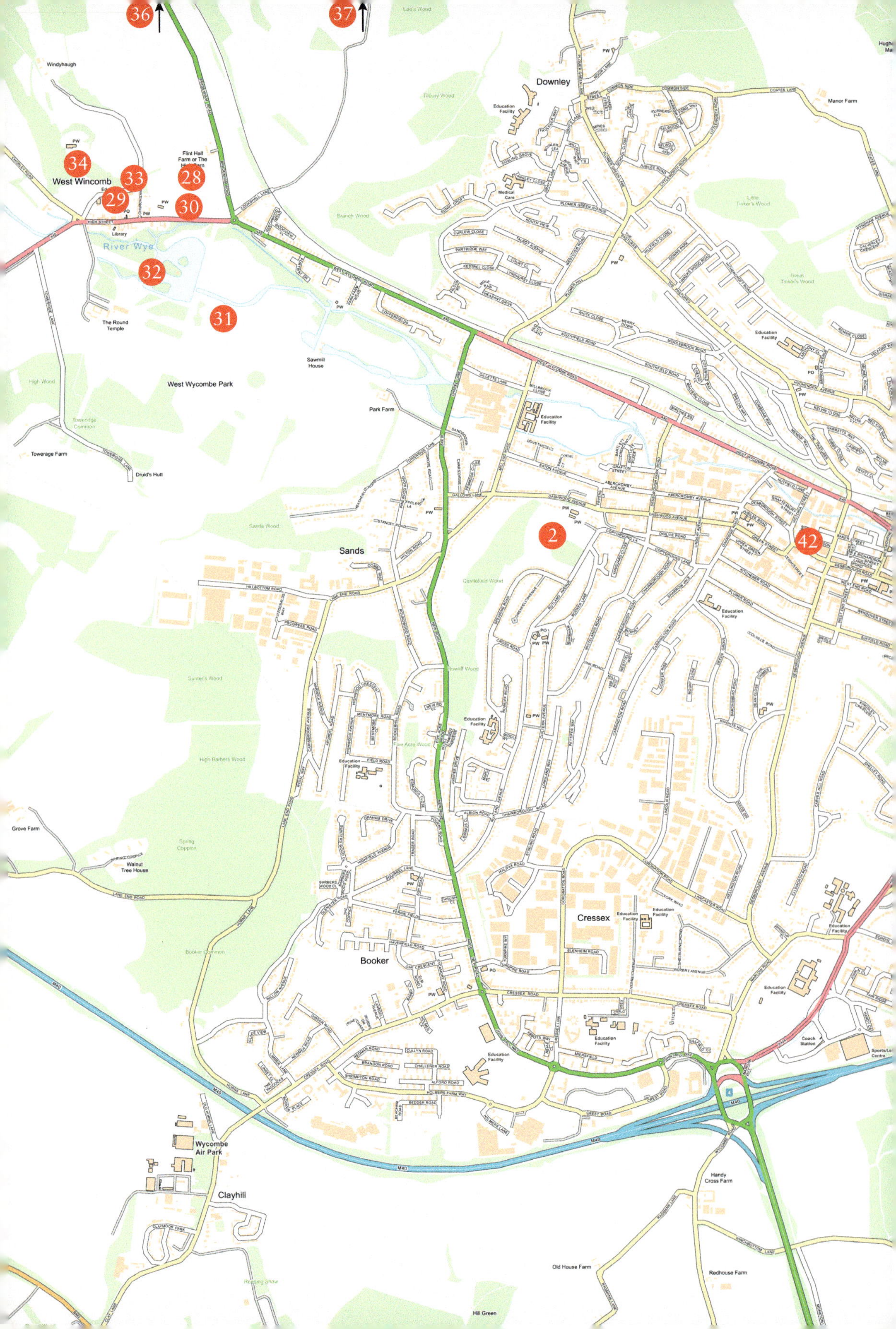

36
37
Windyhaugh
Downley
Education Facility
Manor Farm
PW
34
West Wincomb
33
28
Flint Hall Farm or The
29
30
PO
Library
River Wye
32
31
The Round Temple
Medical Care
Sawmill House
West Wycombe Park
High Wood
Park Farm
Towerage Farm
Druid's Hutt
Sands
2
42
Education Facility
Grove Farm
Walnut Tree House
Cressex
Booker
Wycombe Air Park
Clayhill
Handy Cross Farm
Coach Station
Old House Farm
Redhouse Farm
Hill Green
M40

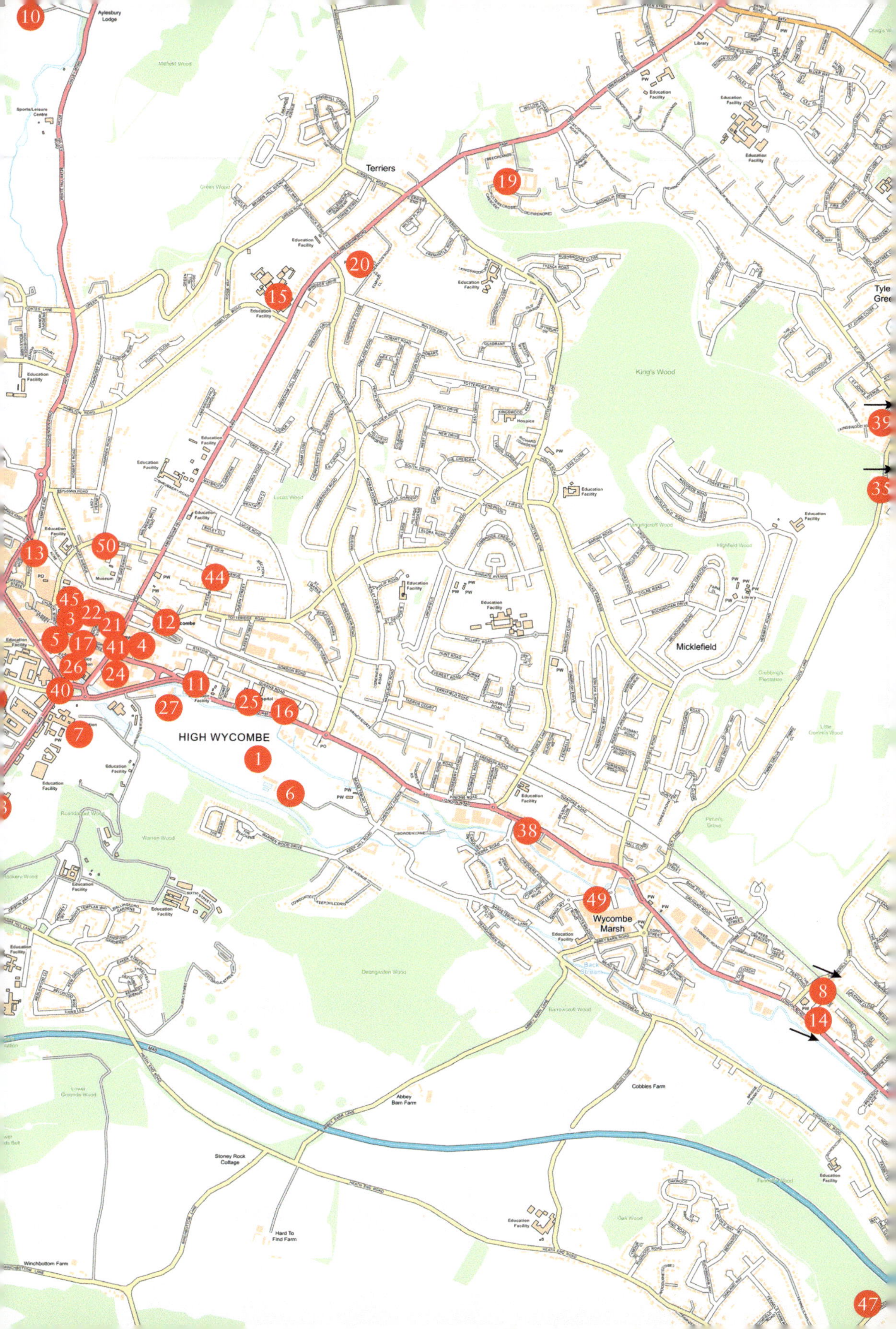

Aylesbury Lodge
Terriers
HIGH WYCOMBE
King's Wood
Micklefield
Wycombe Marsh
Mitchell Wood
Green Wood
Lucas Wood
Warren Wood
Deangarden Wood
Barrowcroft Wood
Cobbles Farm
Abbey Barn Farm
Stoney Rock Cottage
Hard To Find Farm
Winchbottom Farm
Lower Grounds Wood
Oak Wood
Museum
Hospice
Library
Education Facility
Sports/Leisure Centre
Back Stream
10
19
20
15
13
50
44
45
3
22
21
12
5
17
41
4
26
24
40
11
25
16
27
7
1
6
38
49
8
14
39
35
47

# Key

1. Roman Villa
2. Desborough Castle
3. All Saints Church
4. Hospital of John the Baptist
5. Guildhall
6. Bassetsbury Manor
7. Wycombe Abbey Scool
8. Burleighfield House
9. Hughenden Manor
10. St Michael's Church, Hughenden
11. Trinity United Reformed Church
12. High Wycombe Railway Station
13. Clock House
14. St Peter's Church, Loudwater
15. Royal Grammar School
16. Nags Head
17. Little Market House
18. Castle Hill House
19. Magdala House/De Havilland House, Terriers
20. St Francis' Church, Terriers
21. Wheatsheaf Inn
22. Red Lion Hotel
23. Rupert Gates
24. Town Hall
25. Union Baptist Church
26. Wycombe Swan Theatre
27. Pann Mill
28. West Wycombe Hill Fort
29. West Wycombe Mausoleum
30. Church Loft
31. West Wycombe Gardens
32. West Wycombe Park
33. Hell Fire Caves
34. St Lawrence's Church, West Wycombe
35. Holy Trinity Church, Penn
36. Bradenham Manor
37. RAF High Wycombe
38. Brands House
39. St Margaret's Church, Tylers Green
40. St Mary Street
41. Crendon Street
42. Grand Cinema
43. Rex Cinema
44. Palace Cinema
45. Odeon Cinema
46. Loakes Park
47. Loudwater Station
48. Oxford Road
49. Wycombe Marsh Paper Mill
50. Priory Road/Church Street

# Introduction

High Wycombe lies some 30 miles to the north-west of London within the beautiful, rolling countryside of the Chiltern Hills. It is often looked upon as a modern, provincial, home counties town and a satellite of London. It is a view expressed by many who know little of Wycombe's history, and initially discover it by way of its 1930s suburban housing estates, which dot and crowd the town's surrounding hills. It would be the wrong impression.

The history of High Wycombe goes back before the Romans stepped foot in Britain, and, despite its modern expansion, contains reminders in its architecture of a past which includes the Iron Age, Saxon and medieval, Georgian, Victorian modern. It is, architecturally speaking, a town for all seasons.

The name High Wycombe is first mentioned in AD 799, during the Saxon period, when it is recorded as 'Wichama' from the Old English 'wic' and 'ham', which probably have the same denotation meaning 'settlement', 'village' or 'home'. By AD 970 the settlement had become Wicumun. The word 'cwm' is Brythonic and means 'valley' or 'combe'. There are other theories put forward by place name experts who have suggested that the name could refer to the Latin word 'Vicus', meaning 'farm', and a Celtic word used by the Romano-British for fellow Celts, 'Cym'. The word is still used today in the ancient name of Wales, Cymru. 'Vicuscym' may well have been the Roman word for the British farm in the valley. Today the name has evolved into High Wycombe – the valley of the River Wye high above the Thames.

The buildings and structures of a town are said to be the fingerprints of all who have lived in or passed through throughout its history. The architecture of those who have left their mark on Wycombe can be found in and around the town. However, one can also discover evidence of the ever-changing nature of the town's development with continual alteration and rebuilding.

Much of old Wycombe has succumbed to redevelopment; ancient streets, medieval alleyways and fondly remembered stores and shops have given way to the needs of the motor car. Yet, realistically, it has probably always been so. The High Wycombe of the fifteenth century was a vastly different place to the eighteenth-century town, and so it goes up to the present day. Happily, there are still many old Wycombe buildings to be enjoyed to show us what an attractive and historic place it still is.

The fifty buildings in this book are divided into four sections. Buildings in High Wycombe include surviving structures dating from the Iron Age through to the modern era. Buildings in West Wycombe detail the many fine houses in this village on High Wycombe's doorstep. Buildings near Wycombe include houses and churches outside the town, but which have been connected with the history of the borough. Lastly there are those buildings which no longer stand, yet despite their destruction and redevelopment, they remain fondly in the memories of many townsfolk, and also give us a perspective on where High Wycombe is in the twenty-first century.

# The 50 Buildings

## 1. Roman Villa

It may seem odd to include a building which no longer exists, at least on the surface, in a book on the architecture of High Wycombe. Yet, the Roman villa that once stood on the Rye is far too important and significant to leave out when we come to understand the history of the town.

The Romans arrived in Britain in AD 43 with the invasion of Emperor Claudius. Over the following 400 years they defeated, subdued and eventually assimilated the native British tribes into the Roman empire. By AD 150 they had become secure enough to build their grand villas in their newly won land, and were attracted, as many people are today, by the beauty of the Chiltern Hills. Evidence of Roman occupation has been found in the Wycombe district at Saunderton, West Wycombe and Little Missenden including a Roman road that followed the line of the modern A40 from Uxbridge to West Wycombe and beyond.

In 1722, workman from the Wycombe abbey estate discovered a mosaic floor and an old Roman pavement on the future site of the Rye and the municipal swimming pool. Although recognising the importance of the find, the mosaic was forgotten until further excavations were carried out in 1863, 1932 and 1954 when it was discovered that the site was a Roman villa of importance.

The villa dates from AD 150–170 and although not luxurious, it was nonetheless solidly built. It was the largest Romano-British villa in Buckinghamshire, and also displayed the earliest mosaic floor in a building of that date.

The house was 104 feet wide, with wings measuring 70 feet deep, and enclosed by a boundary wall and surrounded by a garden and orchard. The villa consisted of an unusually large and elaborate bath house, which would have been far too big to be solely for the use of those living in the house. It has been speculated that such a large bath complex suggests that the villa must have been at the heart of a working farm. The later history of the villa is obscure, although it is known that the building was still standing in the fourth century when alterations were carried out.

Curiously, the mosaic, which was discovered in 1722, is not the one that was unearthed in the 1954 excavations. It is possible that more evidence of the villa is to be found if archaeologists are given the chance for further digs. Yet this may prove difficult as early excavations, particularly those in the eighteenth and nineteenth centuries resulted in considerable damage to the site . The site of the villa was also used as an allotment for a time. Today, the site is occupied by a swimming pool.

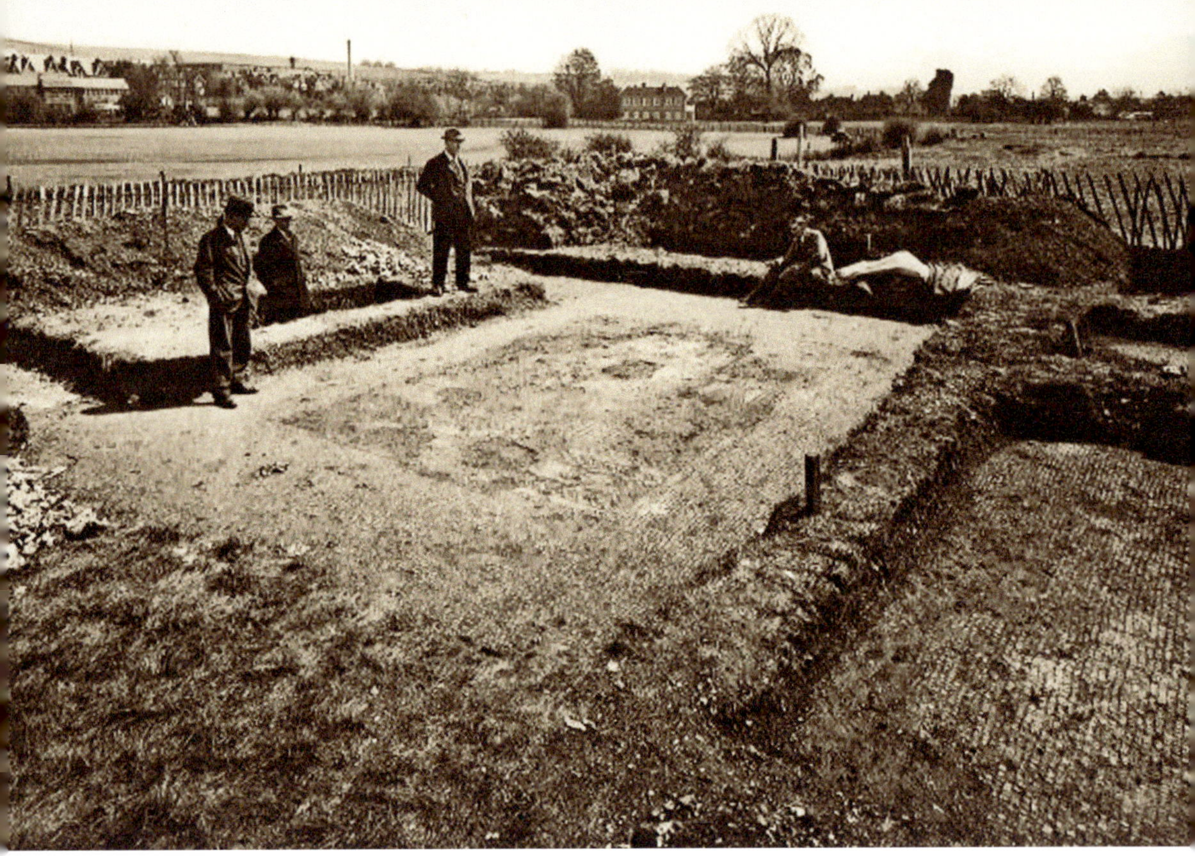

*Above*: Excavations of the villa site in the 1930s.

*Below*: What the villa might have looked like in the fourth century AD.

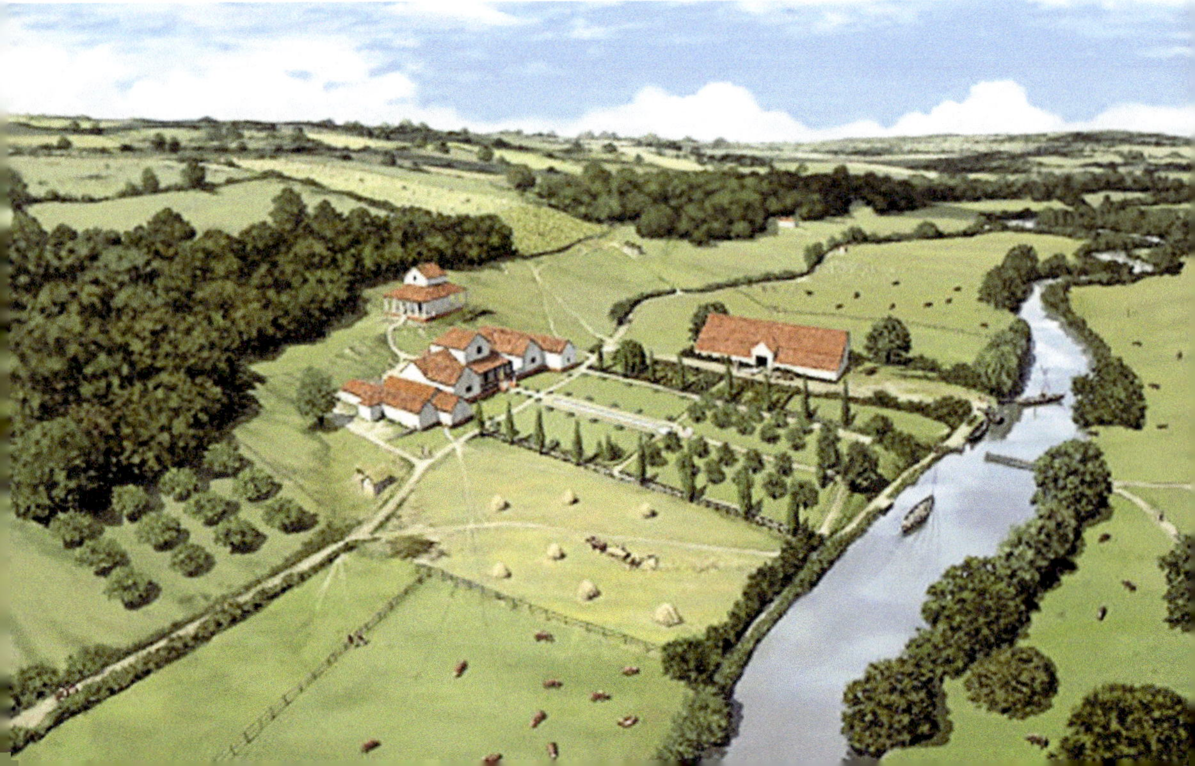

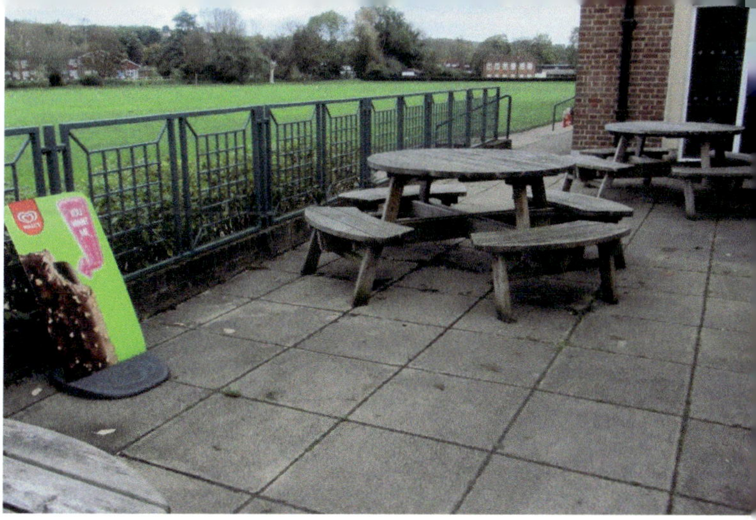

High Wycombe Lido now stands on the site.

## 2. Desborough Castle

Some years ago I lived next door to a couple who were newly arrived in Wycombe. One pleasant day they told me they were off to see the castle. I naturally assumed they meant Windsor as it is relatively close to the town. Soon after, they returned and said they couldn't find it. Which castle were they looking for I asked? 'Desborough', they replied.

What my neighbours were looking for, of course, was a traditional castle of turrets, towers and a drawbridge. It is what we expect a castle to be. Yet, in the strictest sense of the word, Desborough is indeed a castle. The word is taken from Latin 'castellum', meaning 'fortified place'. Its history goes back into the mists of time, and was, at one time, a fortified place. However, there are other fascinating puzzles about Desborough, and if my friends had only known it, they missed out on exploring one of Wycombe's most intriguing locations.

Desborough Castle is situated in a most incongruous location for it sits on the edge of a housing estate on the south side of the town; a place one would not expect to uncover ancient history, yet archaeological digs have revealed that the site has been used for thousands of years and the valley has been an important route through the Chilterns from at least the Bronze Age.

There is some confusion as to whether the site was at one time an Iron Age hill fort. Remains of ramparts and ditch fortifications, along with part of a lynchet (the evidence in raised furrows of centuries of ploughing), suggest that it was a Bronze Age defensive position.

Records also reveal that during the twelfth century it was used during the civil war between King Stephen and Empress Matilda. The castle was the property of Stephen's brother, Henry of Blois, and was probably besieged by the forces of Matilda. It is known that King Stephen was at the siege of Wycombe in 1139, and although it has been thought that the siege took place at Castle Hill in the centre of the town, Desborough seems the more probable location. The site is an ideal position to control the valley and the road to Oxford.

Perhaps the most intriguing and puzzling of finds unearthed at Desborough are those which point to contact with merchants from the ancient world. Two Greek coins, one gold, bearing the image of Philip of Macedon (Alexander the Great's father) were uncovered. The other was a bronze coin from Ambracia, in western Greece, dating from between 238 and 168 BC. Roman coins have also been discovered.

In 1743 traces of a Roman building were discovered, as was a stone window frame from a medieval church, yet no further trace of these structures has yet been unearthed. It would seem that Desborough Castle has more secrets waiting to be revealed by archaeology.

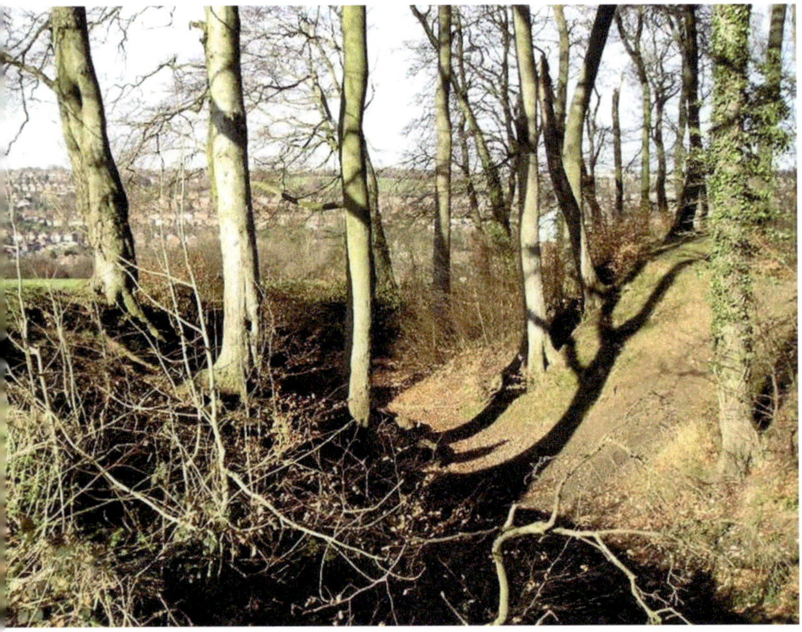

The ramparts of Desborough Castle.

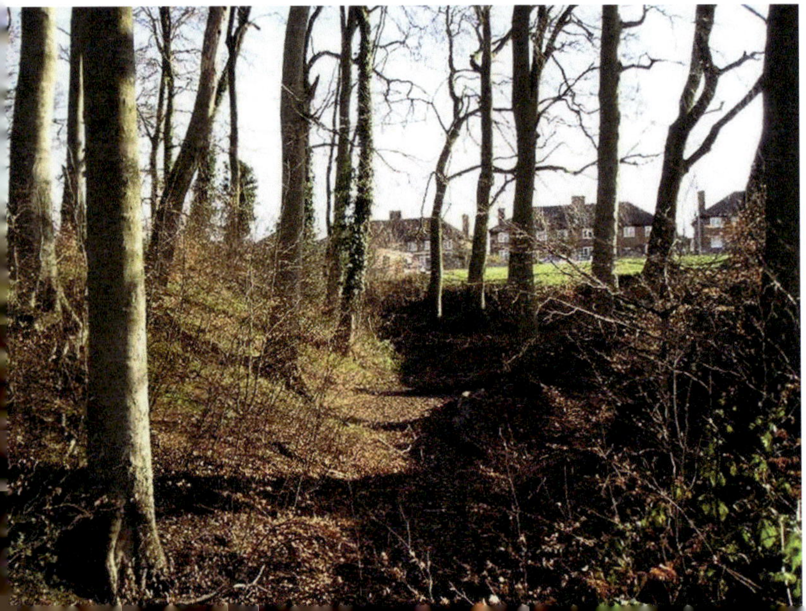

Council houses sit cheek by jowl with the castle defences.

## 3. All Saints Church

The church of All Saints in the centre of Wycombe has the distinction of being one of the largest town churches in Buckinghamshire. It has a spacious and impressive six-bay nave, central crossing, side chapels and a solid west tower that rises some 30 metres.

There was probably a place of worship on the site as far back as Saxon times, yet the church we see today was founded in the Norman period, and consecrated by St Wulfstan, Bishop of Winchester (1062–95) However, as with most churches in England, it has been altered and added to over the centuries. The architecture we see today is late thirteenth century. The original central crossing tower was pulled down in 1509 and rebuilt at the west end. The upper part of decoration with quartrefoiled parapets and pinnacles was added in 1755 and designed by Henry Keen, who, two years later, designed the Guildhall in the high street (see Guildhall).

The church's chief monument was erected in 1754 and stands in the north chapel. It is of Henry Petty, Earl of Shelburne, who died in 1751. It is a magnificent piece of work and truly worthy of a cathedral. It depicts the earl dressed in the garb of a Roman centurion, with members of his family adorned in togas. Its fashioning illustrates how the rich and powerful of Wycombe viewed the Church of England in the eighteenth century.

Although the church is chiefly thirteenth century, the interior is a Victorian restoration of 1873, as is the exterior, which was restored in 1887. Most churches underwent renewal and refashioning in Victorian times following the Gothic Revival.

The Gothic Revival dates to around 1840, and was the Victorians desire to return churches to a medieval appearance. If we could return to All Saints in the reign of HenryVIII we would be shocked at the appearance of the interior. It was a riot of colour; it was everywhere, on statues, mouldings, walls, hangings and windows. A giant screen (the rood), topped by a statue of Christ, separated the nave from the chancel. There were numerous alters throughout the church with their own lamps burning. The dim lighting, smell of incense and the coming and going of chanting priests created an atmosphere of mystery and awe.

Following the Reformation and the establishment of the Protestant Church of England, in 1547, during the reign of Edward VII, all superstitious idolatry, popery and iconography was ordered to be removed. The celebration of the sacrament gave way to the sermon, and churches became plain and dour unadorned preaching boxes.

However, by the nineteenth century the Industrial Revolution had transformed the country into a belching, choking factory. The Victorians looked to the past and the medieval period as a romantic idyll, and restored churches to a pre-sixteenth-century appearance. The church we see today in its bones is medieval, but in layout and appearance is a Victorian building.

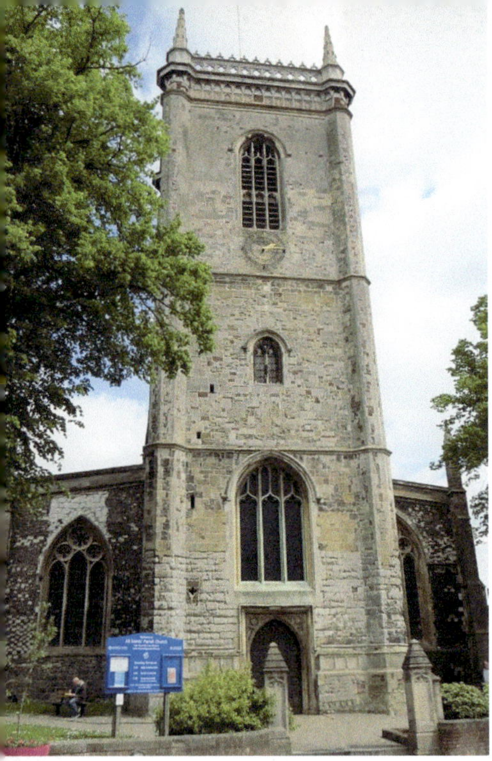

*Left*: The fifteenth-century tower of All Saints Church.

*Below*: The nave of All Saints.

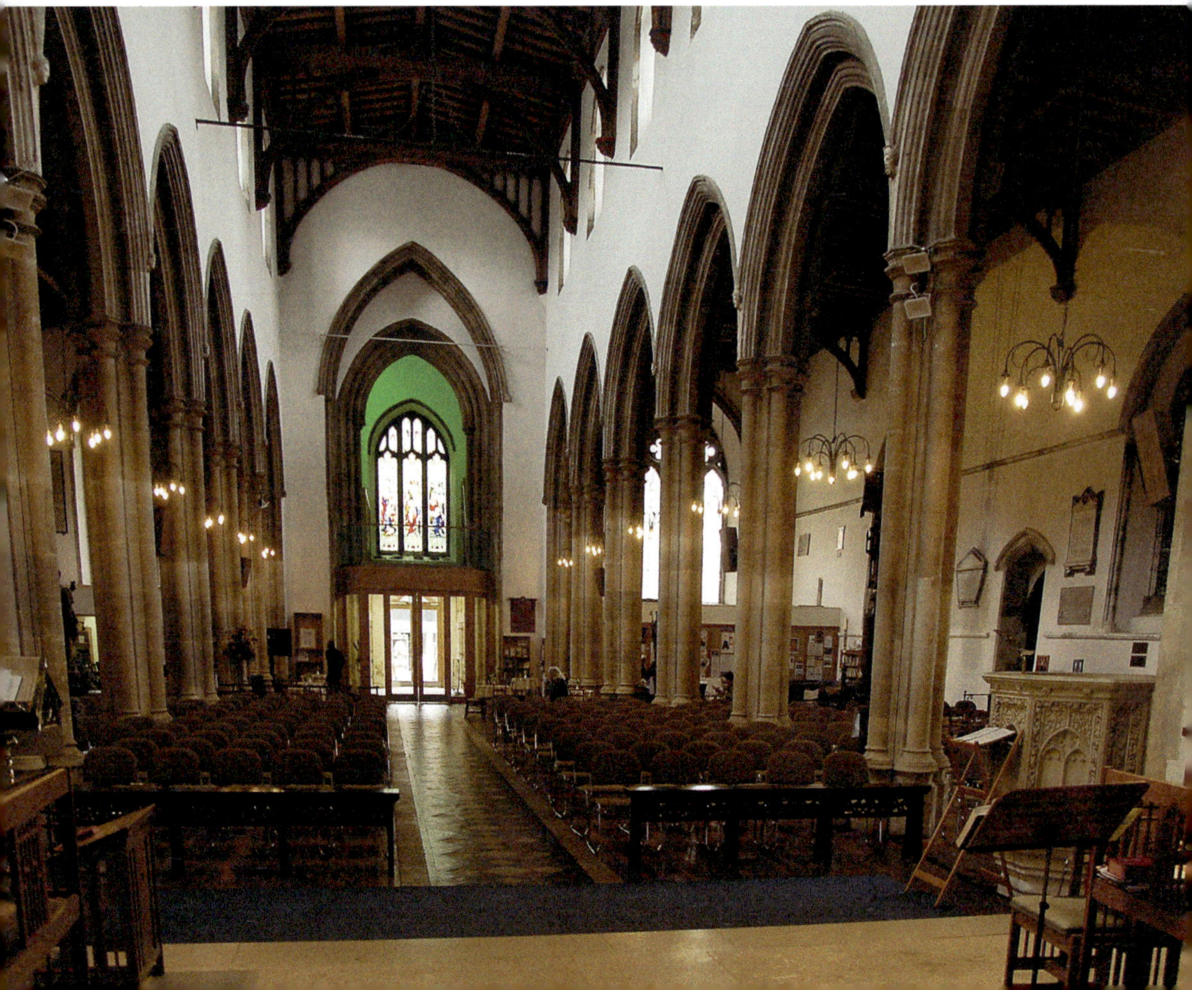

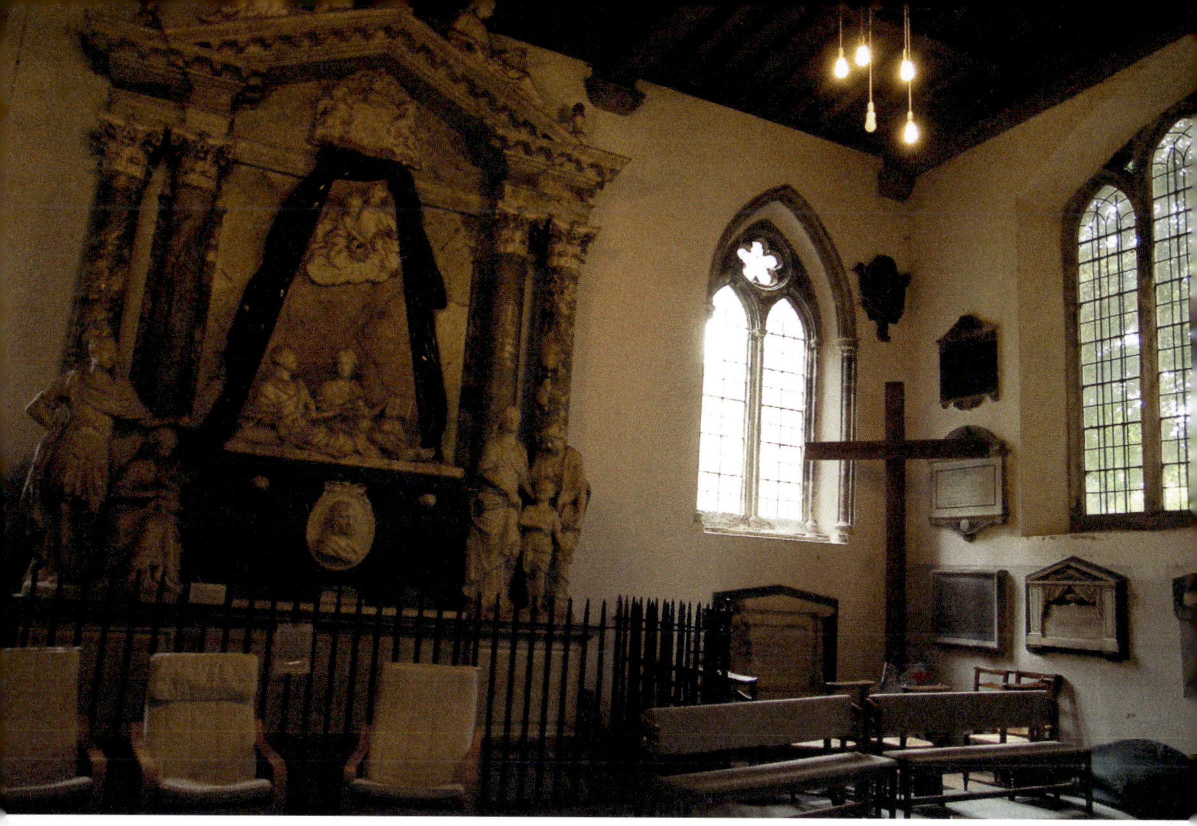

The Grand Shelburne Monument.

## 4. Hospital of St John the Baptist

Despite being a ruin and just a fragment of its once substantial size, the Hospital of St John the Baptist can claim to be Wycombe's oldest standing structure. It dates from 1180 and consists of a ruined infirmary, hall and a chapel. It is constructed of flint and stone dressings, and the four aisles of the main ruin display rare surviving twelfth-century architectural features such as sturdy round piers and unmoulded arches. This style of building, known as Romanesque or Norman, was the standard throughout the twelfth century. However, the remains of the chapel also show two Gothic windows from the thirteenth and fourteenth centuries, suggesting that the hospital was developed throughout its history.

The full extent of the hospital is unknown and remains such as collapsed walls may exist below ground within a raised area to the east of the site, and under the present line of the adjacent Easton Street. In 1767 part of the original building was demolished to widen the road.

The importance of the ruins is that they are a rare example of a medieval hospital surviving in a town. Some 800 hospitals are known to have existed, but only the location of the larger ones is known, and very few of these have been subject to archaeology. During the early thirteenth century it was staffed

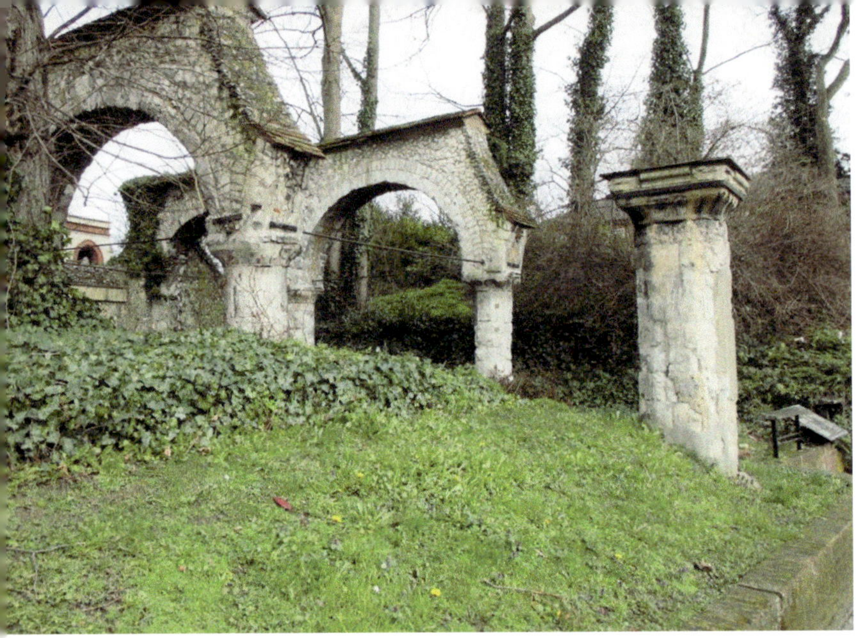

The scant remains of the Hospital of St John.

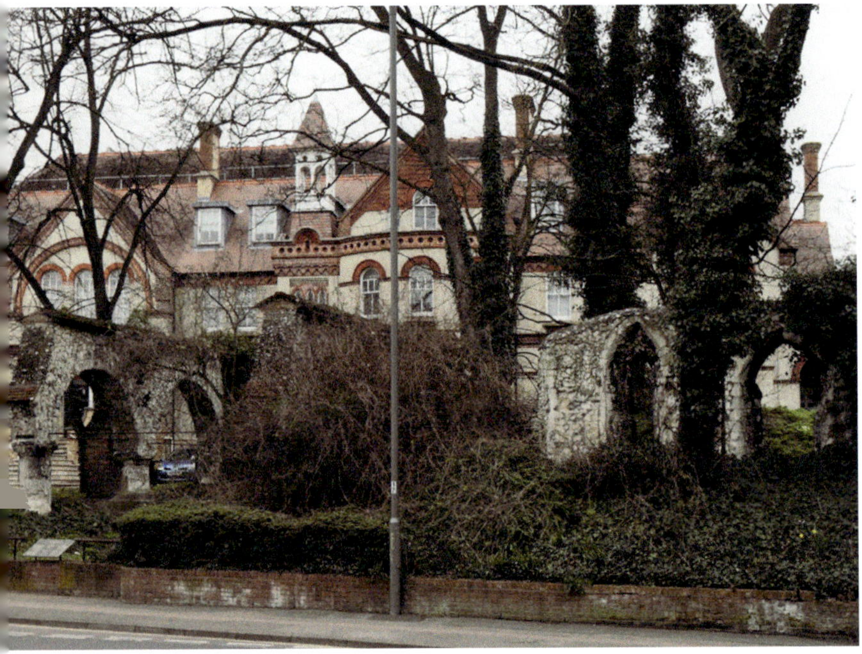

The ruins of the hospital, with the Old Royal Grammar School in the background.

by a master monk and lay brothers and sisters who cared for the poor and infirm and also accommodated those passing through the town. By 1344 the hospital was in the patronage of the mayor and burgesses of Wycombe in which capacity it remained until it was dissolved in 1520 during the Dissolution of the Monasteries.

In 1550 the hospital was used as a school. The remaining poor and infirm patients were moved to almshouses, which were built opposite. Incredibly these houses survived until 1970 when they were demolished. In 1562 the newly formed school received a royal charter from Queen Elizabeth I, and became known as the Royal Grammar School (see Royal Grammar School).

Many Wycombe residents pass by these 'pile of stones' every day and give them little thought. Yet they are an essential part of Wycombe's history. In the ever-changing face of the buildings in Wycombe it seems a miracle, even in their ruined form, that the hospital survives. Next time you pass, stop for a moment and contemplate the building you see. Step inside and think that when the hospital was built in 1180 the Kings of England spoke French, the services in the chapel were conducted in Latin and the people of Wycombe spoke English, which would be incomprehensible to us today.

## 5. Guildhall

If High Wycombe has a true centre, then it is arguably the Guildhall at the end of the high street. It was built in 1757 by Henry Keene as a gift from the Earl of Shelburne, who, at the time, resided in Wycombe Abbey. It consists of two storeys with an open ground floor with Tuscan arcading. Its classical grandness reflects the prosperity of Wycombe during the eighteenth century. During the nineteenth century it was designated the Town Hall and its upper rooms were used for council and committee meetings.

Reference to a guildhall in Wycombe goes back to at least the early fifteenth century. In 1604 a new market house, or guildhall, was constructed opposite the entrance to the Chilterns shopping centre in Chapel Street. It was half timbered and stood on twenty-two wooden posts, which no doubt created a covered market and meeting space below. Henry Keene's designs for the present guildhall were based on the same idea. The common prison was located in the dungeons below the old guildhall, and remained as such before Newlands police station was built in 1817. Incredibly, Wycombe's original fifteenth-century guildhall survived until it was demolished in 1930.

The same fate might well have occurred for the present Guildhall. Astonishingly, in 1850 there were proposals to demolish it as it was deemed a traffic hazard. Happily, despite the redevelopment of the town centre, it has survived and quite rightly so. Along with All Saints Church, it is, in my opinion, Wycombe's most beautiful building.

The Guildhall is the scene of perhaps the town's most celebrated ceremony: the weighing of the mayor. The High Wycombe mayoralty is the only one of its kind in the world where its mayor and all officers get weighed every year. The event, which has its origins in medieval times, takes place each May. When a new mayor and his officers and staff begin their year in office, each is weighed on scales outside the guildhall and the weights recorded. If by the following May, when they are once again weighed, they are found to have put on weight, they are booed by the townsfolk for becoming fat at the expense of the ratepayers.

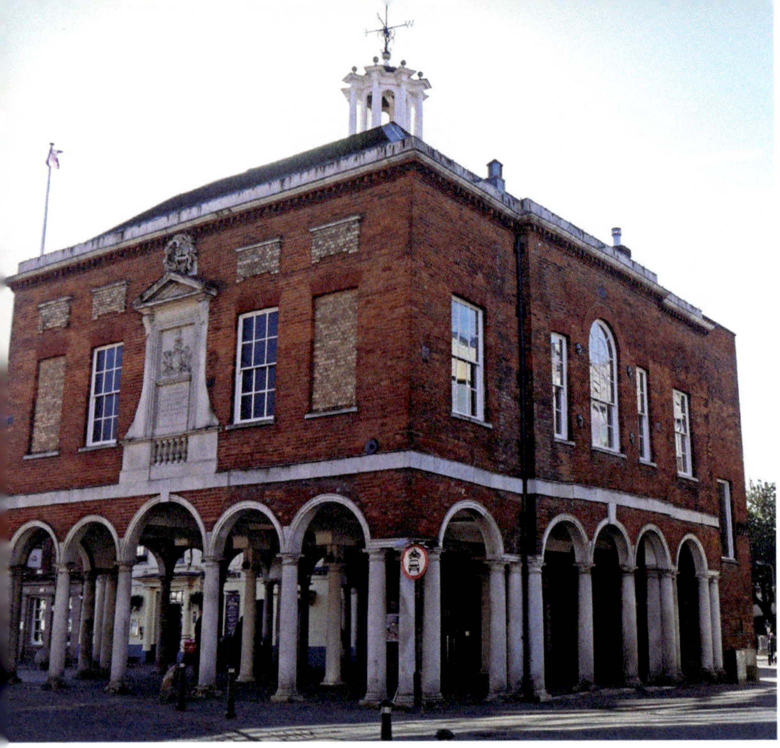

The stately red-brick Guildhall.

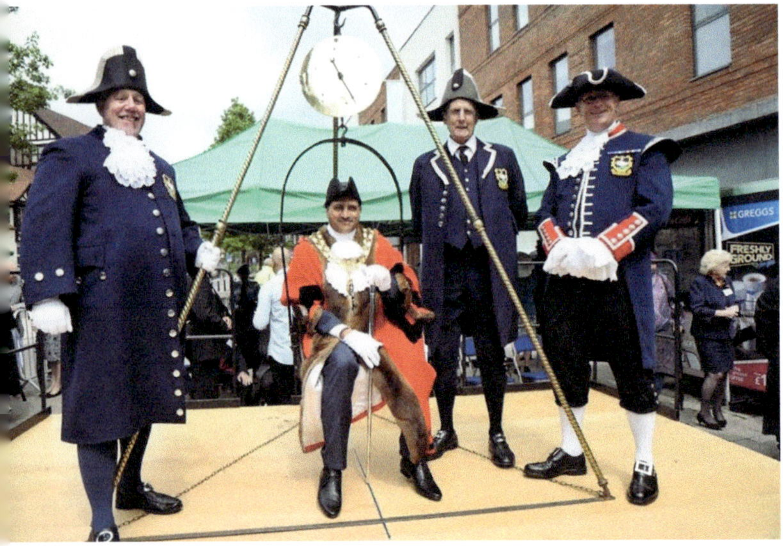


The ceremony of weighing the mayor.

## 6. Bassetsbury Manor

Bassetsbury Manor dates back to at least the thirteenth century when it was granted to Alan de Basset by King John in 1205. Basset was at Runnymead, on the banks of the Thames, in 1215 when the king was forced to sign the Magna Carta (the Great Charter), which was an early point on the road to democracy and the curbing of the monarchs power.

Alan de Basset seems to have been a troublesome man, for it is recorded that during his time as lord of the manor he engaged in numerous legal battles with the burgesses of Wycombe over rights and privileges, one of which was his right to collect all the animal dung deposited in the streets of the town. However, despite being one of the nine barons who witnessed the king's seal on the Magna Carta, he seems to have not fallen out with the monarch, for John was a guest at the manor on three occasions.

Of course, the building we see today didn't exist in the thirteenth century, although it probably stands on the same site as Alan de Basset's house. Like many of England's ancient manors, Bassetsbury passed through a number of families down the centuries. In 1281 it was the property of the Despencer family. Some fifty years later in 1332 it passed to William de Bohun, Earl of Northampton. By the late fifteenth century it came into the hands of the Dashwoods of West Wycombe. During the Tudor period a half-timbered house stood on the site, which was owned by John Raunce, who's wealth and social standing must have been considerable for he entertained Queen Elizabeth I at Bassetsbury.

The house was remodelled in the late seventeenth century and its possible that the building we see today incorporates some of the earlier structure. The Flemish bond of the walls, the chimneys and the brick surrounds suggest a date before 1640. From the early eighteenth century ownership reverted back to the Dashwoods. Between 1812 and 1828 it became the royal Lancastrian school housing 180 boys. In 1883 it was sold to Lord Carrington, who must have neglected the building for by 1920 it was almost derelict and in desperate need of repair with no internal sanitation, water or lighting. It is no wonder that when wartime leader Sir Winston Churchill visited the house with a view to buy it, he declined.

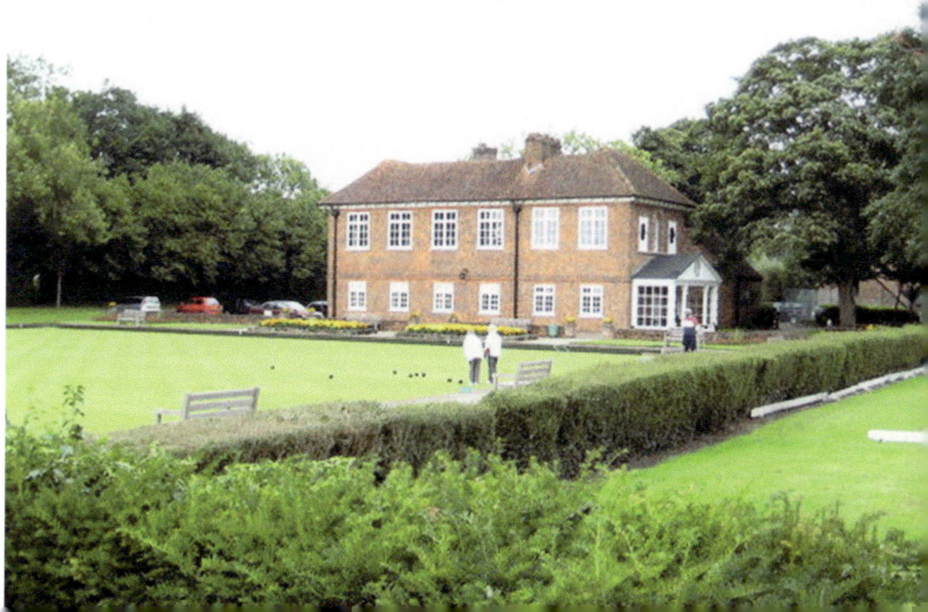

Bassetsbury Manor, which is now a private school.

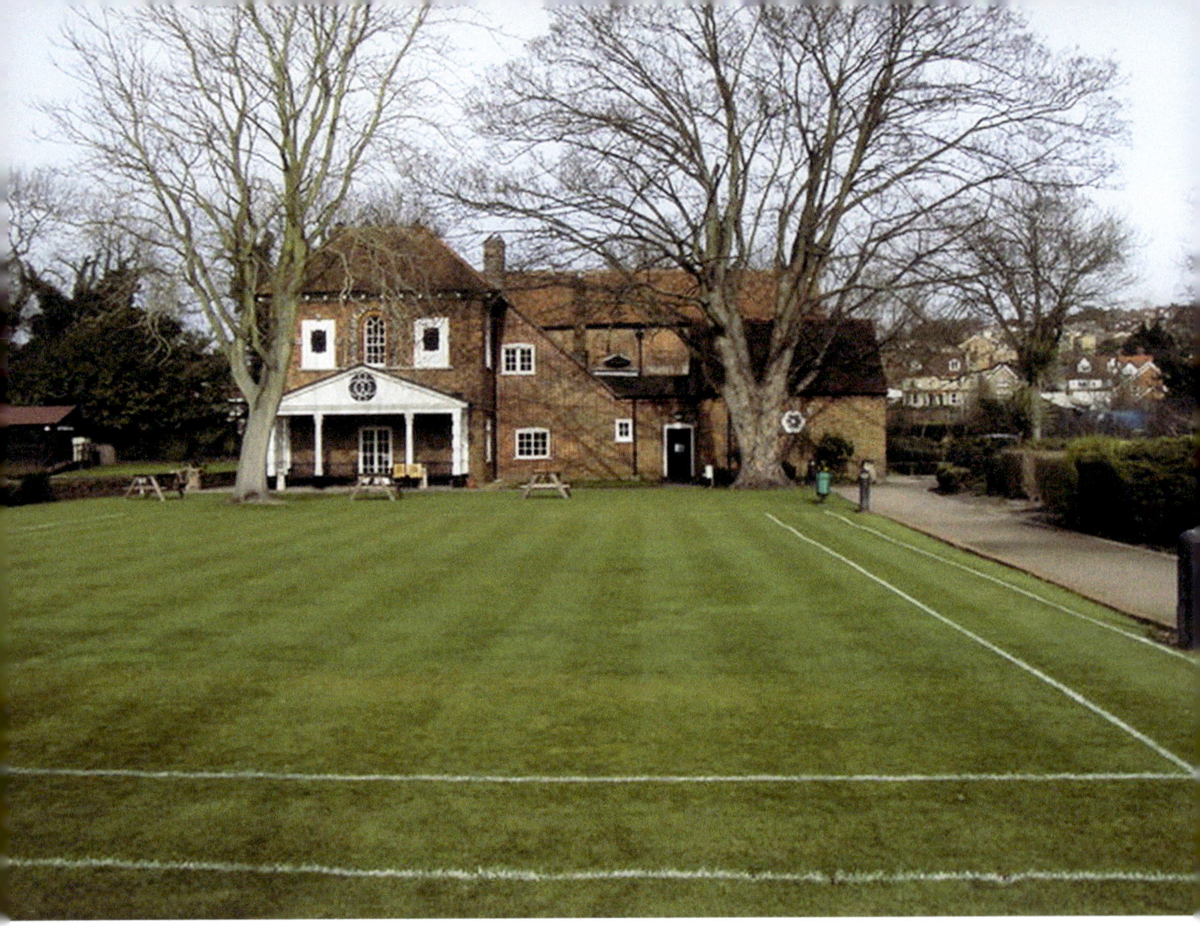

The manor might well have been home to Sir Winston Churchill.

The house today really owes its survival to local furniture maker Fred Skull. He restored the building throughout the 1930s to its seventeenth-century appearance, but retaining some of its Tudor origins. The main doors to the manor and several other fittings (including wood panelling) came from the original Quaker Meeting House in Crendon Street when it was demolished. When renovation was complete the house was refurbished with period furnishings and antiques. It must have been an impressive sight, for in 1934 Queen Mary visited Bassetsbury to view the restored house.

In 1952 the contents of the house were auctioned and the building and estate purchased by Wycombe District Council. The building was sold by the council in 2014 to be converted into a private school, in which capacity it remains today.

## 7. Wycombe Abbey School

The origins of the site of Wycombe Abbey go back to the thirteenth century when the land was part of the holding of Godstow Nunnery in Oxfordshire. It is possible that some form of dwelling stood on the site at that time. However, by the early seventeenth century the site was occupied by Loakes manor house. In 1605 it was the property of William Jackson, yet over the following hundred years passed through numerous hands until in 1700 it became the home of Henry Petty, 1st Earl of Shelburne.

When Petty died in 1753 he bequeathed the estate to his nephew, John Fitzmaurice, who embarked on an ambitious building program. Architect Henry Keene (see Guildhall) renovated the manor by adding a three-storey building to the existing house.

In 1761 the manor was inherited by the 3rd Earl of Shelburne, who employed master landscape gardener Capability Brown to improve the grounds. Shelburne would later become Prime Minister from 1772 to 1773. The Shelburne family rarely visited their Wycombe home, preferring their Wiltshire estate. However, during their time the house was visited by many prominent figures such as, John Wesley, Benjamin Franklin and Dr Johnson.

In 1798 the house was sold to Robert Smith, 1st Lord Carrington. In 1803 he employed architect James Wyatt to remodel the manor in the then fashionable Gothic style. To complement the house's new medieval appearance the name was changed to Wycombe Abbey, although the building was never a religious establishment, unlike Lacock Abbey in Wiltshire, which was once a monastery and following the dissolution was converted into a stately home for William Fox Talbot, the inventor of photography.

In 1896 the Carringtons sold the house and part of the grounds to a syndicate to form Wycombe Abbey School. Accommodation for pupils were constructed together with a sanatorium, a substantial brick and concrete classroom area, chapel and a dining room. The school would later expand with the acquisition of the old Carrington home, Daws Hill House. In 1942, during the Second World

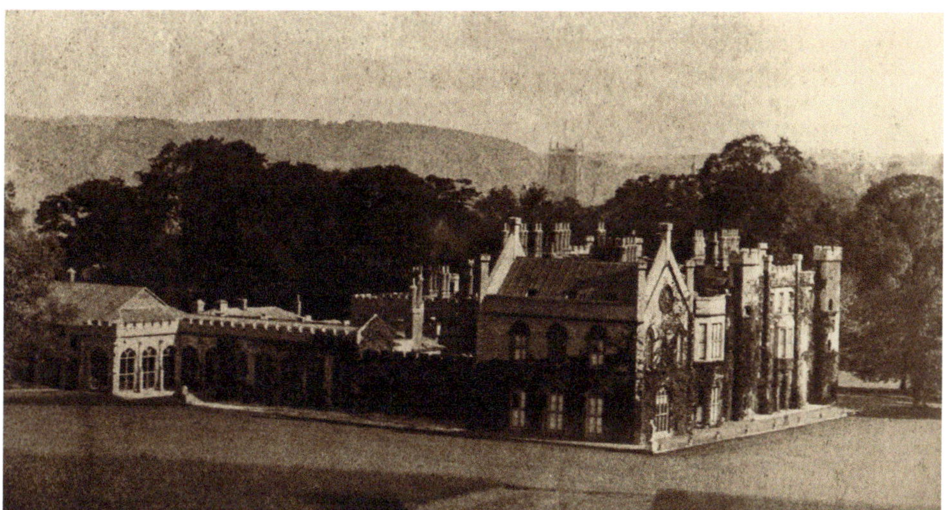

Wycombe Abbey in 1896.

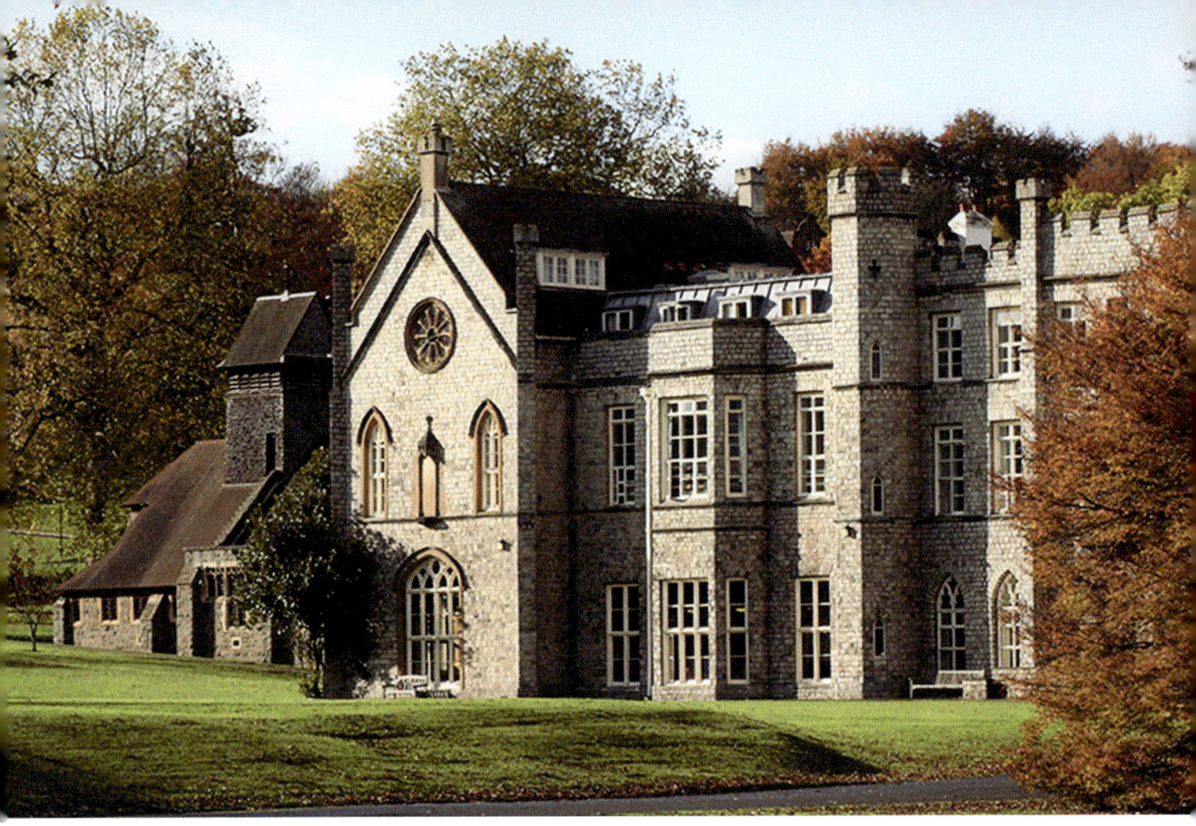

A modern view of the Wycombe Abbey.

War, the school was requisitioned by the Air Ministry to serve as the headquarters of the United States Eighth Air Force. In July 1946 legendary American band leader Glenn Miller and his orchestra played at the abbey.

## 8. Burleighfield House

Those readers who often drive through Loudwater and negotiate the roundabout for either Tesco superstore, the M40, or straight on to Holtspur and Beaconsfield may be unaware that behind the trees adjacent to the junction stands a grand Victorian mansion that has a curious past.

Burleighfield House is a substantial twenty-room residence set in 3 acres of grounds that back on to open countryside. It was built in 1860 by Thomas Burch Ford, a wealthy Loudwater Mill owner. Burch Ford, although a successful businessman, was also a supporter of the welfare of the local community as well as the working conditions of his employees. He was also a man of strong religious views and built a private chapel within the grounds of his house.

When he died in 1892, the funeral took place in his chapel before his coffin was taken to Wycombe for burial. It was a lavish send-off, for the procession stretched over a quarter of a mile as it proceeded through Loudwater, Wycombe Marsh and on to the town.

Following Burch Ford's death, the house became in turn the home of a leather goods manufacture, a guest house and a private school. In 1960 Burleighfield achieved a moderate level of fame when it became the home of master stained-glass designer Patrick Reyntiens. He established the Burleighfield Arts school and studios. It was Reyntiens who designed the stained glass for Liverpool cathedral, Christ Church, Oxford, and the baptistery at Coventry Cathedral.

By 2003 the studios had run into financial difficulties and was put into liquidation. Thereafter the house remained unoccupied until 2005 when it taken over by a Yellow Pages publisher. The property was in a bad state of repair with many of the rooms needing complete refurbishment. Today, the house has been restored and is home to a number of small businesses.

The author has a special fondness for Burleighfield as, before becoming a writer, and between 2005 and 2010, I was employed there as a caretaker. A grand Victorian mansion set in pleasant, landscaped grounds was a pleasing place to work until I discovered that the house had another, sinister aspect: it was believed to be haunted. A ghostly, evil-looking woman in black was said to walk the house and the grounds. On several dark winter mornings I would walk alone up the driveway to the darkened house to open up and commence work. Making my way through the rooms, along the shadowy corridors and up the stairs was always with trepidation. Would the woman in black leap out on me? I was glad when the staff arrived and I had company.

Today Burleighfield's future remains uncertain. Plans have been submitted to demolish this fine Victorian mansion and build a number of houses on the land. Let's hope that common sense can prevail and this essential part of Loudwater and Wycombe history is preserved.

The front of Burleighfield House.

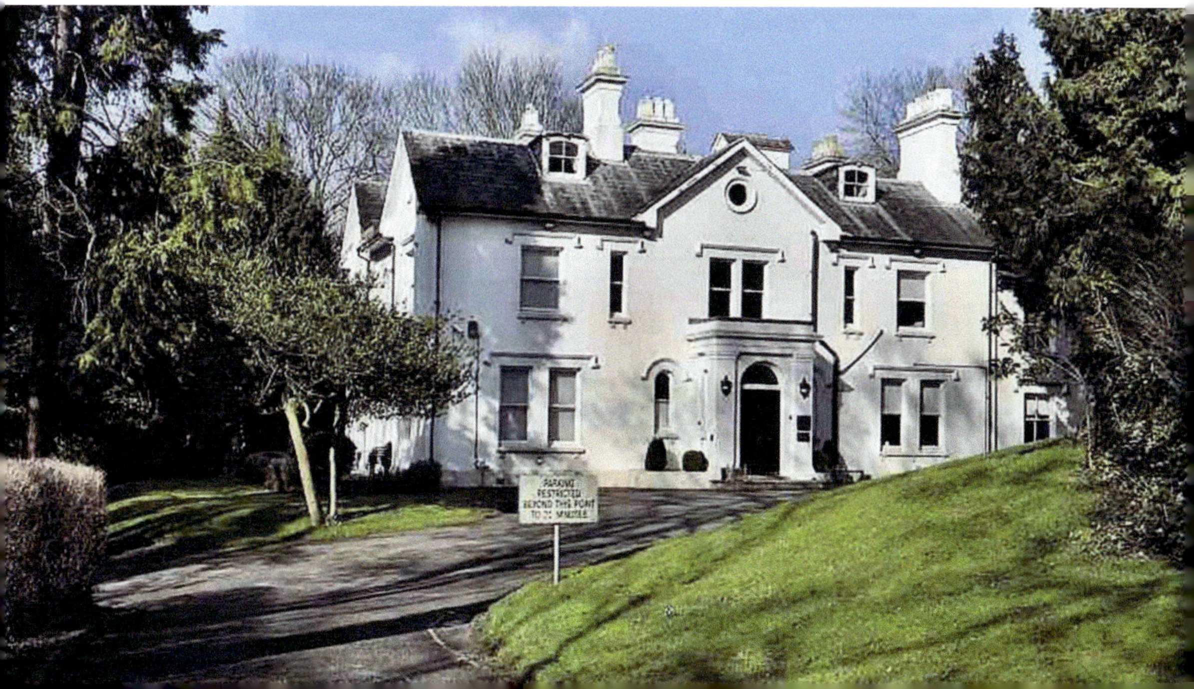

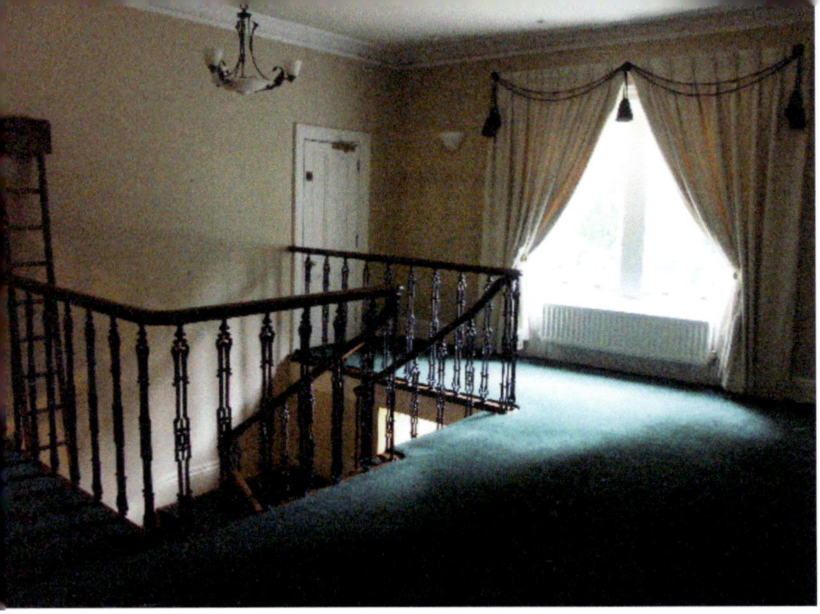

The central staircase.

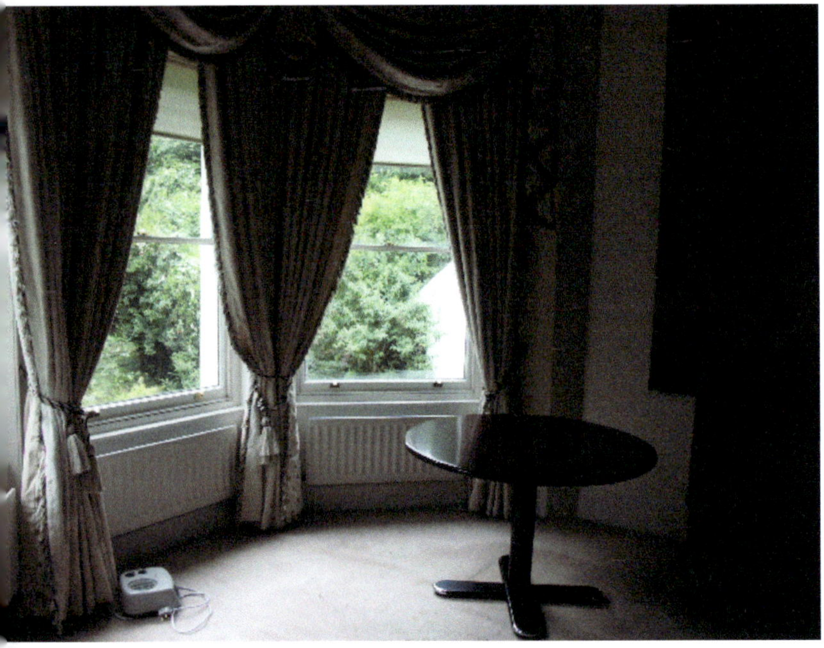

One of the rear rooms, which looks over the back gardens.

## 9. Hughenden Manor

Hughenden Manor stands just outside the centre of High Wycombe, and today is mostly known as the former home of Victorian politician and statesman Benjamin Disraeli, who lived there from 1847 until his death in 1881. The manor of Hughenden is first recorded in 1086, and, although not certain, it is possible that a house occupied the site in the fifteenth century. During the sixteenth and seventeenth centuries it was the property of the Dormer family. However, from

1737 it was owned by the Savage family, who began to develop an existing farmhouse into a modest house of three storeys.

In 1847 the house was purchased by Disraeli, who was a favourite of Queen Victoria. He became Prime Minister in 1868, and again between 1874 and 1880. He bought the house with a loan of £25,000, equivalent to almost £1.5 million today, from two political allies. It was necessary for Disraeli to be seen as a wealthy landowner to further his political career. The statesman remodelled the exterior and interior manor in the Gothic style, although the exterior is in a mock-Jacobean brickwork.

Under Disraeli's care, the building was transformed into a Victorian red-brick house decorated with fanciful pinnacles. Hughenden was Disraeli's home from 1848 until his death in 1881.The house interior underwent many changes after Disraeli's death, but several rooms have been restored, with many of Disraeli's personal belongings and mementoes displayed as they would have been during his lifetime.

During the Second World War, the house was used as a secret intelligence base code-named 'Hillside' where Air Ministry staff analysed aerial photography of Germany and created maps for bombing missions, including the famous Dambusters raid in 1943.

Hughenden Manor, home to Benjamin Disraeli.

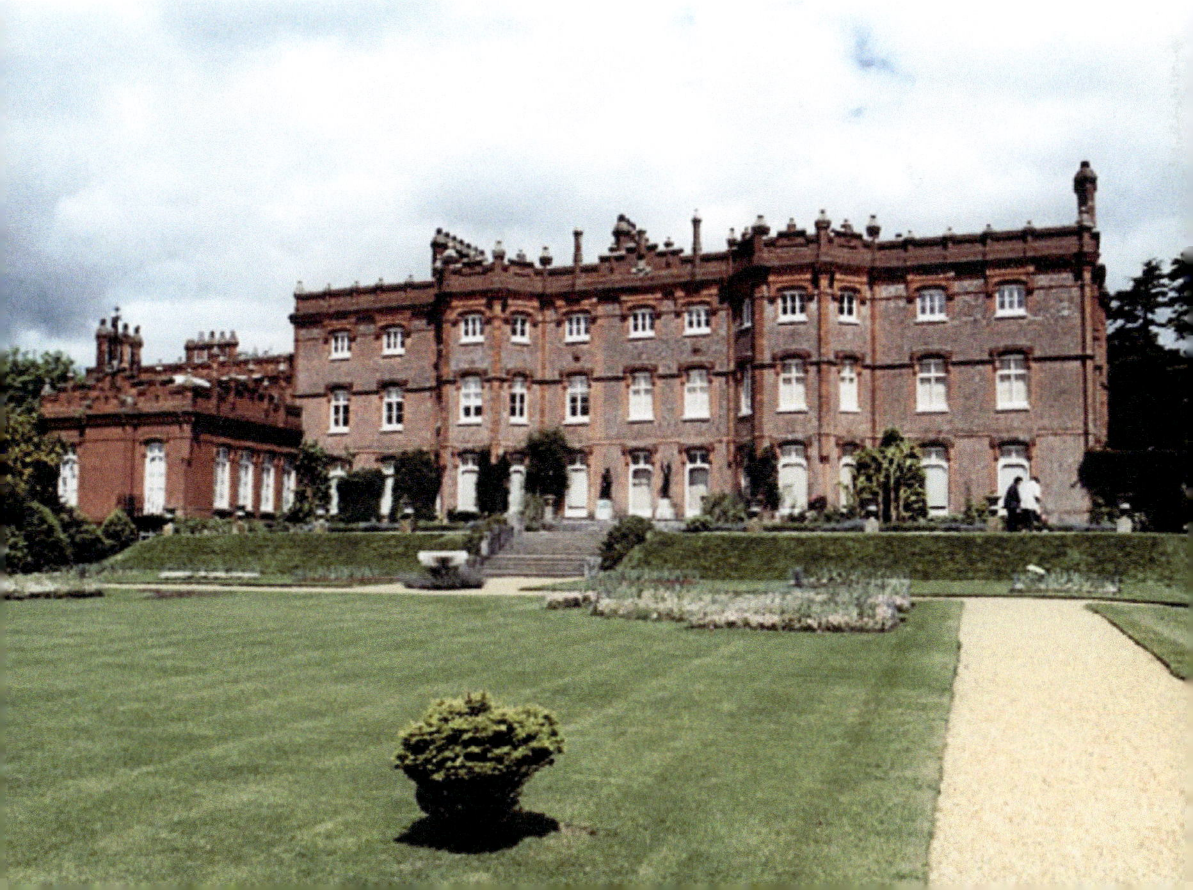

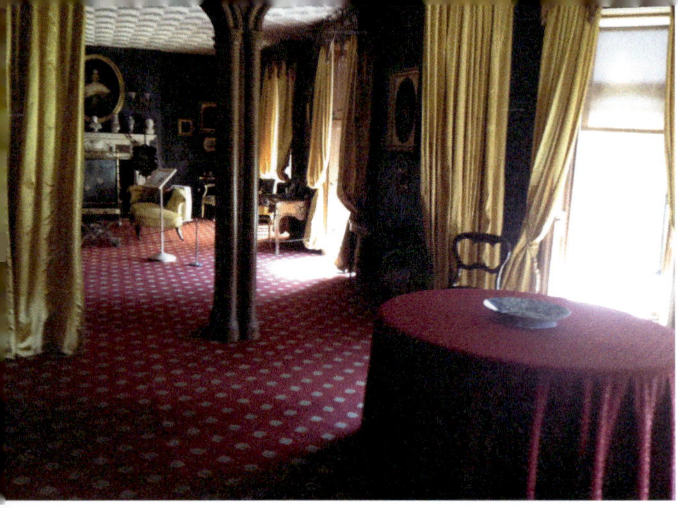

One of the sumptuous rooms with its Gothic arches.

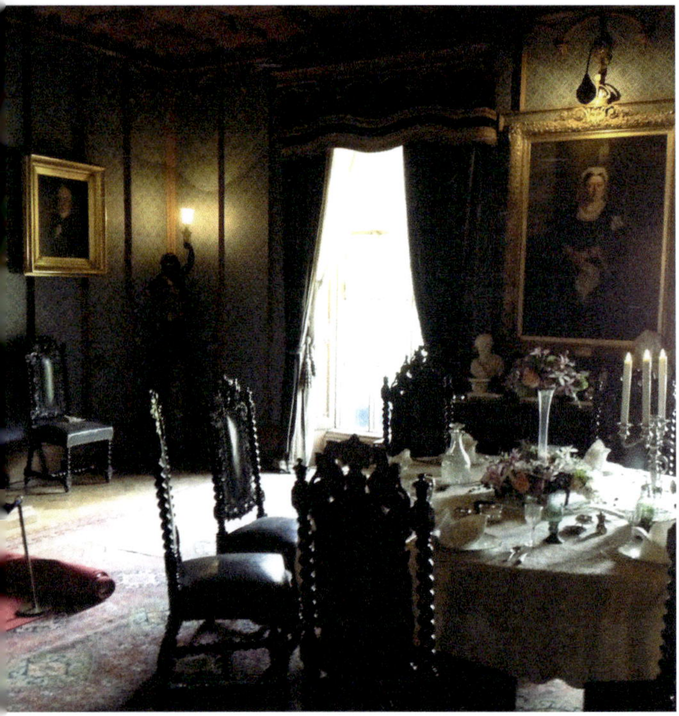

A table laid out fit for the Queen.

## 10. St Michael's Church, Hughenden

The Church of St Michael sits in a beautiful setting just outside the centre of High Wycombe in Hughenden Park, which was once the private grounds of Hughenden Manor (see Hughenden Manor). From 1848 the location became historically linked with Benjamin Disraeli, who was a favourite of Queen Victoria, and also served two terms, 1868 and 1874–80, as Prime Minister of Britain.

Like most churches in England, St Michael's has developed and changed over the centuries. There was probably a place of worship on the site in the twelfth century, established by a one-time lord of the manor, Geoffrey de Clinton. A small chapel was added in the thirteenth century, followed by a nave that was smaller than the present one. Arcading between the north chapel and the chancel was added in the sixteenth century.

By 1870 St Michael's had become almost ruinous and a restoration was needed. Such was the bad state of repair that the church, apart from the medieval chapel, was completely rebuilt. It gave the Victorians of the day their chance to return the appearance of the interior to its medieval origins.

Following the Reformation in England in the sixteenth century all churches were stripped of their medieval and popish superstitious iconography. Interiors were made to look plain with texts from the Bible adorning the walls. However, in 1840 came the Gothic Revival and the desire to return the church to its fourteenth-century appearance; St Michael's was no exception.

The interior, in particular the chancel, is a perfect example of how the Victorians imagined the medieval period of church decoration. It is separated from the nave by a low, open wrought-iron screen. The floor is covered in ceramic tiles and the walls decorated with paintings depicting the nativity. The stained-glass windows cast their garish colour over all. The church is a perfect Victorian setting for the last resting place of eminent Victorian statesman Benjamin Disraeli. His tomb lies outside the church at the east end.

Perhaps the most curious part of the church is the original medieval north chapel. Here one will find effigies of four knights. One is genuine fourteenth-century

The heavily restored exterior of Hughenden church.

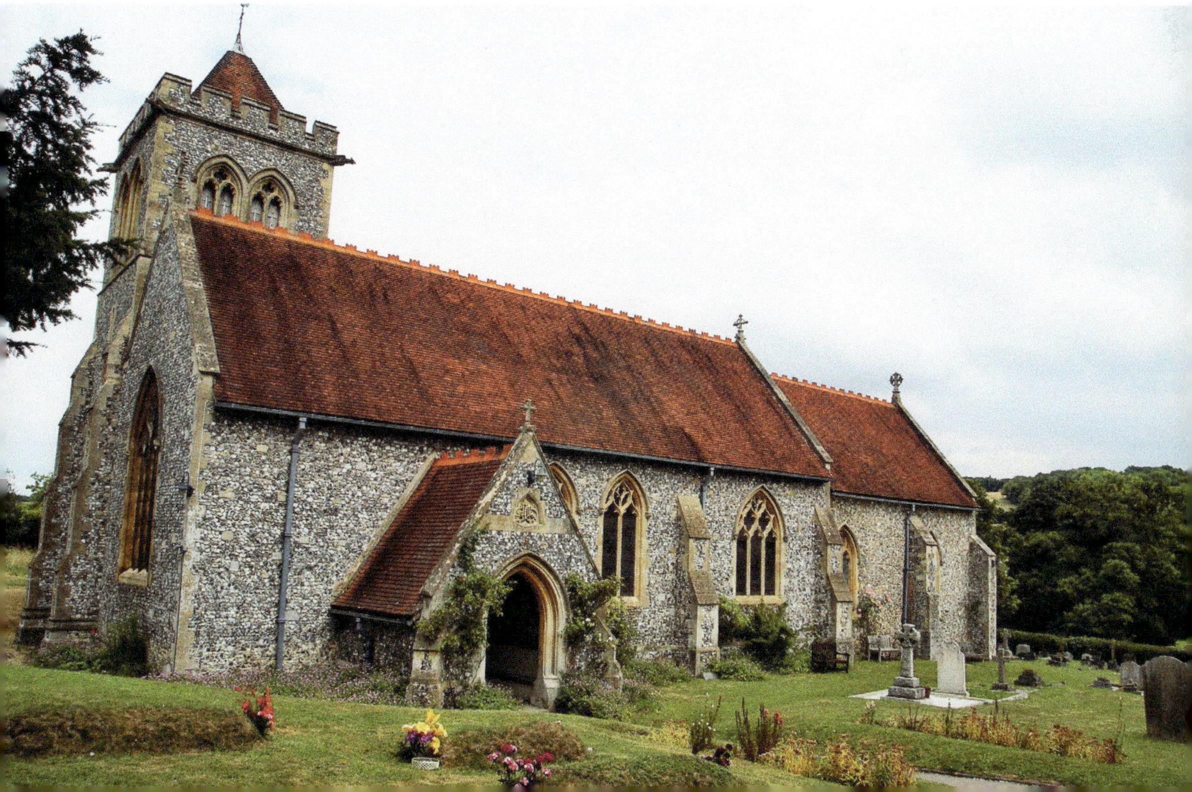

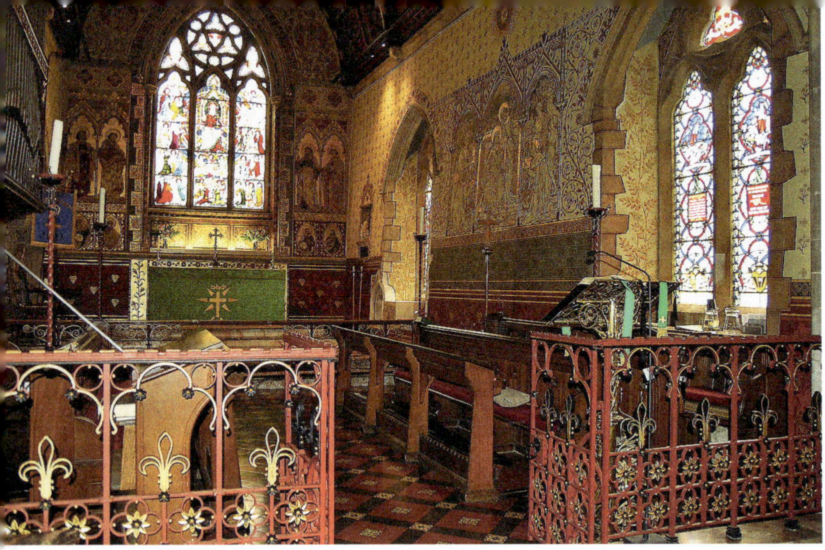

How the Victorians reimagined and restored the chancel.

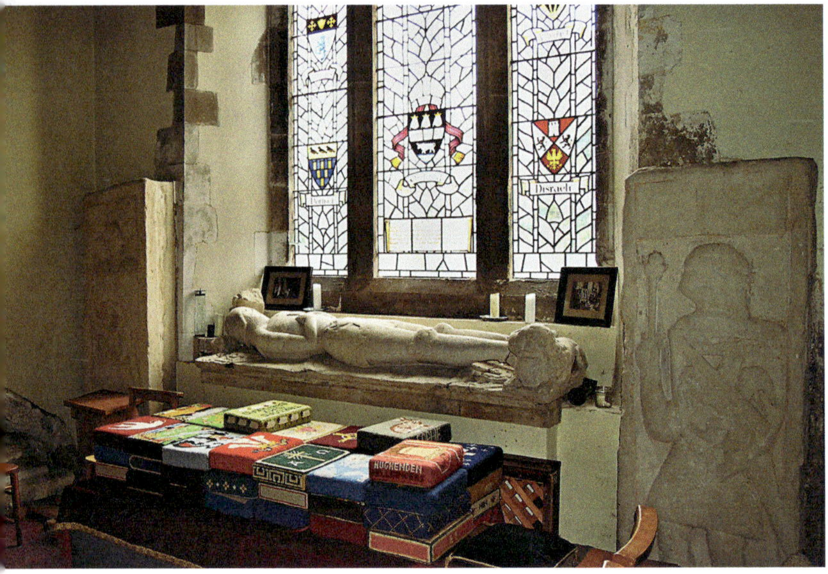

The north chapel showing two of the fake tombs.

work, while the other three, dating from the sixteenth century, are fakes. These were an attempt by the nouveau riche Wellesbourne family to link their line with Simon de Montford, fourteenth-century Earl of Leicester and father of the English Parliament.

## 11. Trinity United Reformed Church

Trinity Church was built in 1850 and was originally called Trinity Congregational Chapel. Congregationalism in Wycombe has its origins in the 1662 Act of Uniformity, which prescribed the form of public prayers, administration of the sacraments and other rites prescribed in the Book of Common Prayer. It sought to abolish many of the religious practises in the Church brought about by the

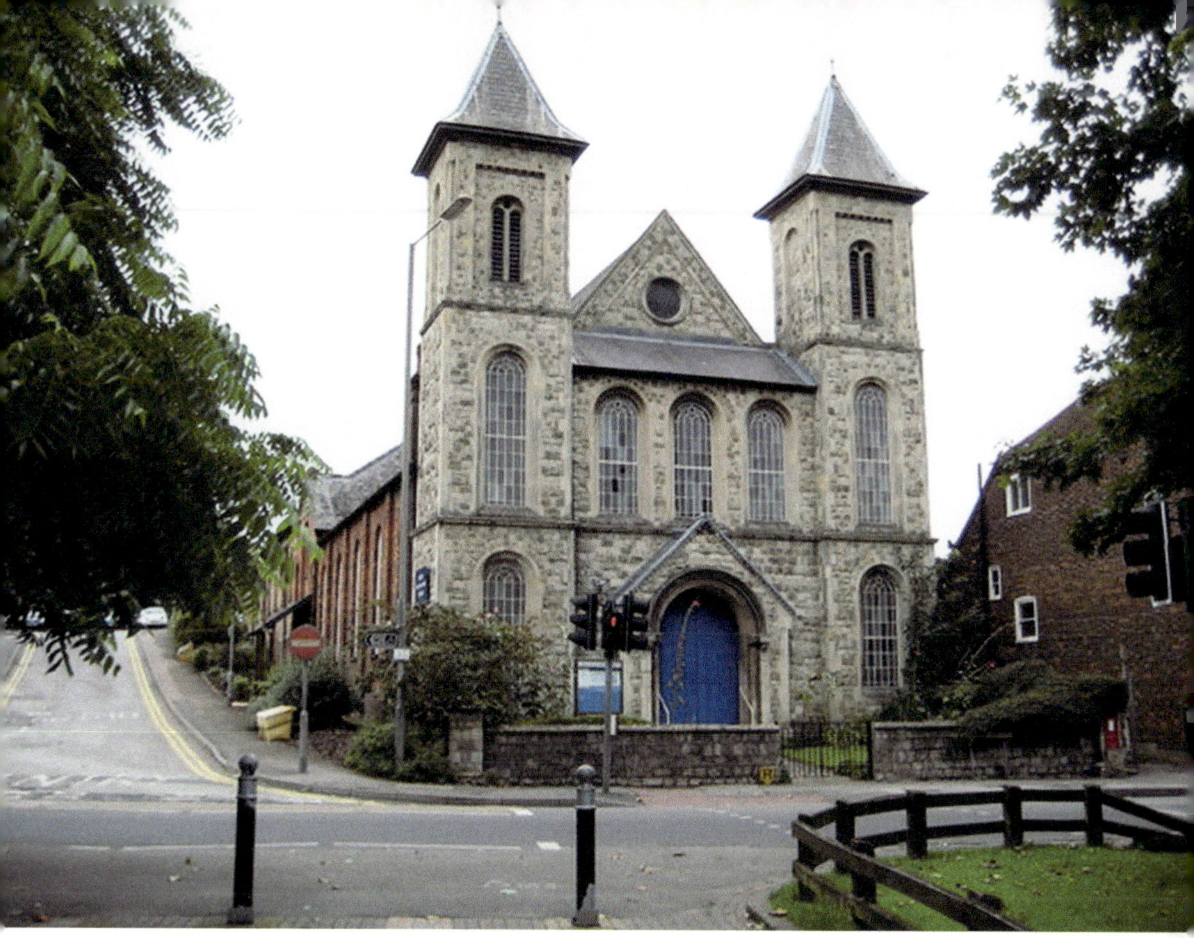

*Above*: Trinity Church was built in a French Romanesque style.

*Right*: The impressive interior with its grand organ.

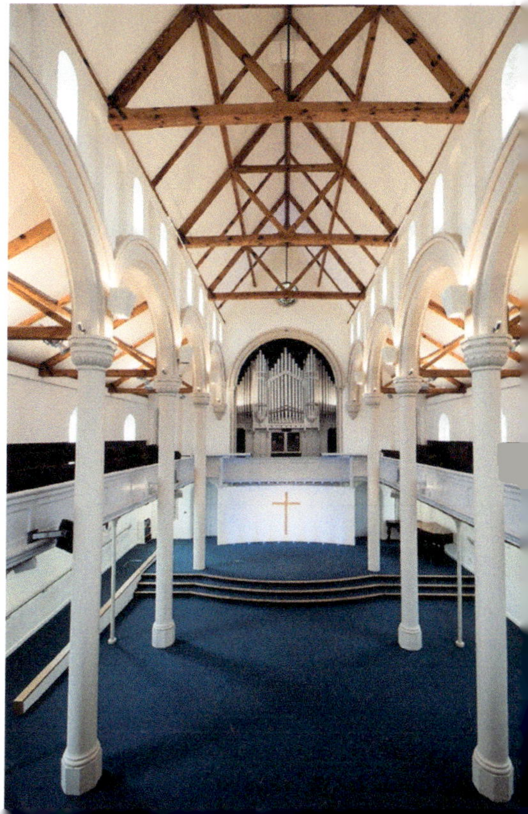

Puritans during the English Civil War. Many clergymen objected to the Act and were ejected from the Church, later to become Nonconformists.

One of those was Revd Samuel Clarke, who established a church in his house in Easton Street where it continued until his death in 1701. Records show that Nonconformists were gathering in a meeting house in Crendon Lane from 1713. In 1779 there was a division among the churchgoers, and some of the members moved to another building in Easton Street. It was in 1850 that they moved into the present site, which now stands opposite Pann Mill.

The church design is interesting as it is built in an almost Romanesque style with a nave, two aisles and two distinctive towers; a church seemingly more at home in France than Wycombe. The interior is light and airy with Romanesque nave columns, galleries and an impressive pipe organ.

## 12. High Wycombe Railway Station

The inclusion of Wycombe railway station might seem an odd choice for a book charting the architectural history of the town. The similar plan and layout of stations across the country reflects a standard design. Wycombe station is no different. However, in saying that we must give exception to the impressive embankment on the stations north side, a wonderful example of bricklaying. Yet the stations importance is not only architectural.

Prior to the first established railway service between Liverpool and Manchester in 1830, many people had to travel long distances by horse-drawn coach. The coming of the railway to Wycombe opened up a new world to the town's residents who had probably never ventured more than a few miles from their homes throughout their lives. Now they could go to London, or further afield. Sociologically and economically it expanded their horizons, and in time would change the demographic of the town as the railway brought new residents.

The first railway station in Wycombe was built in 1854 to a design by Brunel. The station was originally a terminus of the branch line from Maidenhead and was run by the Wycombe Railway until being incorporated into the Great Western Region. Incredibly, the original terminus survives today. The large building is adorned by a giant mural depicting Brunel standing next to an early loco. The station had one platform and a train shed, which covered two broad gauge tracks. On the birdcage walk side of the building was a booking office and waiting rooms.

The station remained in use until 1864, when it was converted into a goods shed. It was at this time that the High Wycombe station we see today was constructed on its present site, allowing for through traffic to the north. The old station was subsequently enlarged and added to over the years until it was taken out of service in 1970. Today it has received Grade II listing as it is only one of six remaining GWR train sheds in Britain.

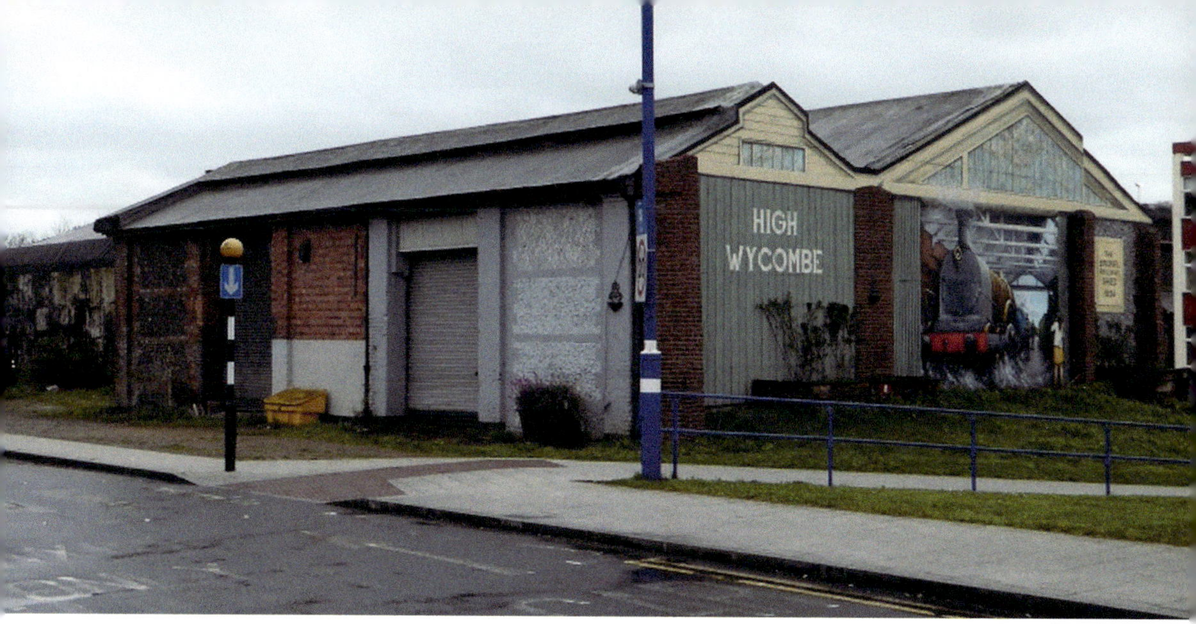


*Above*: The original Wycombe railway station, built in 1854.

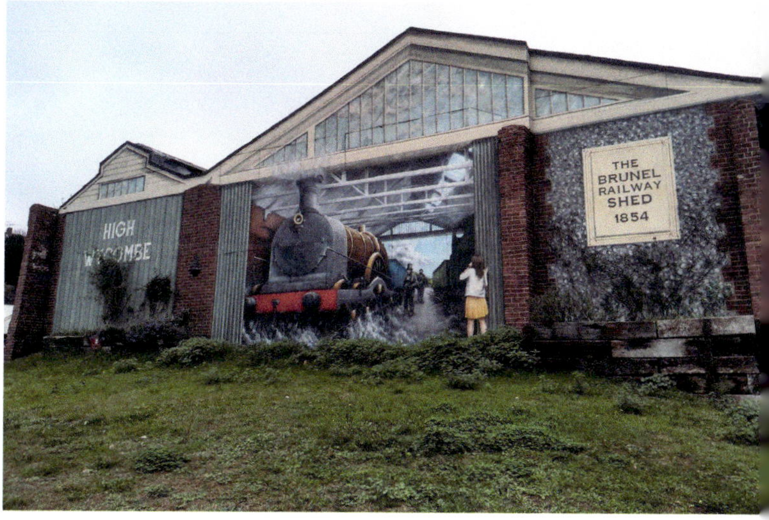


*Right*: The station building was later used as a loco shed.

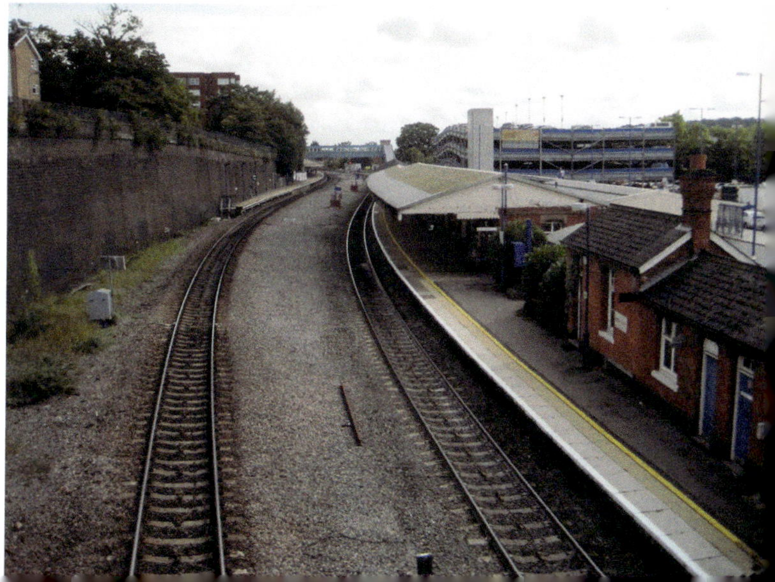

Modern Wycombe station.

## 13. Clock House

Many Wycombe folks probably still refer to this building as the Clock House. There are no doubt others who only know it today as a dental surgery. Yet, this grand, solidly designed Victorian structure started life as the science and arts school. It was built in 1893 at a cost of £2,200, mostly collected by an alcohol tax. The tax, unsurprisingly, was not popular, but was levied to provide compensation for pub landlords who were forced to close when the drinks trade became regulated. Ironically, money raised from those who loved their boozing became available for educational purposes, one of which was the school.

It was opened by Lord Carrington, and contained classrooms, a lecture hall, laboratory, art room and a life room. After the First World War the school played an important part in rejuvenating the town as an official centre for the Ministry of Defence by creating links with local crafts, including furniture making, to help provide training for injured war veterans.

In 1919 the school had begun to outgrow its premises, and moved to the recently vacated Royal Grammar School. By 1925, however, it was decided to close the building and the students operated out of other buildings in Wycombe.

In 1929 the building became a swimming bath until 1946 when it was converted into the town's repertory theatre. Sadly the theatre failed, and the old art school stood unused and derelict until 1983 when it was once again converted into an

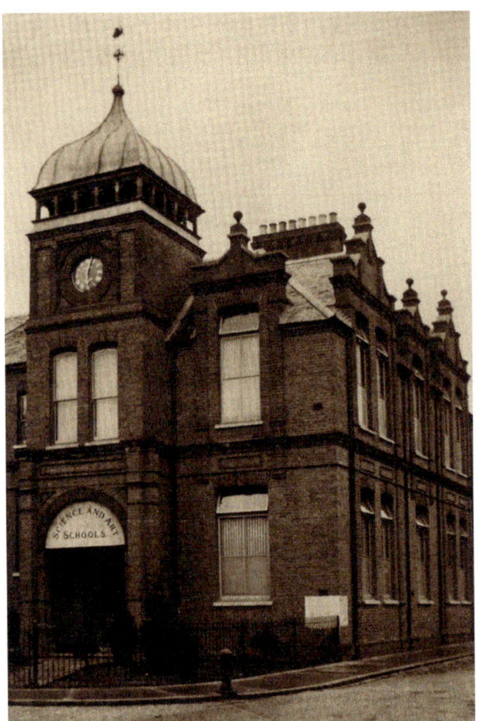


The Clock House on Frogmore.

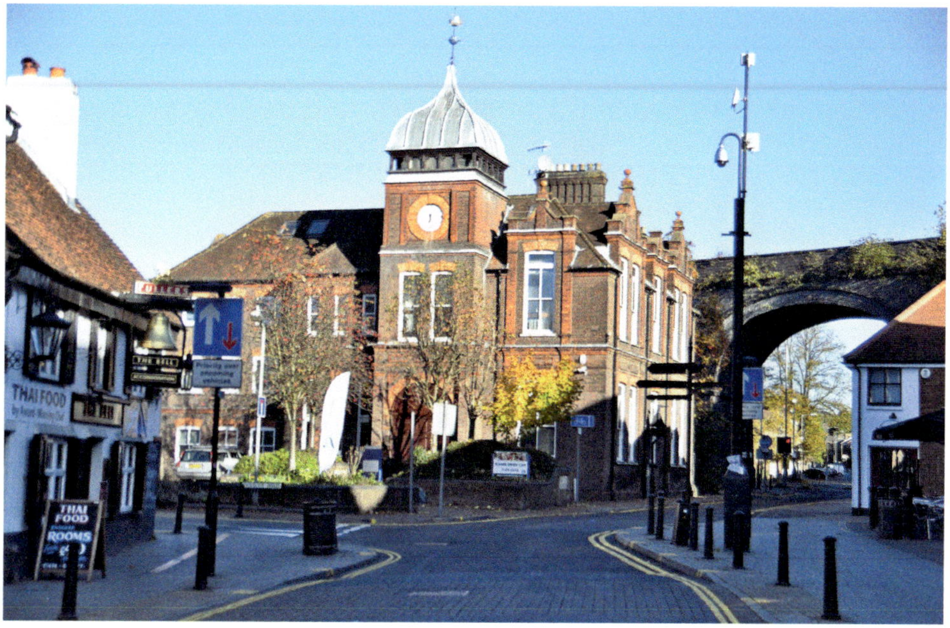


Today the building is a dental surgery.

office block and renamed the Clock House. Today its role has changed once more, this time into a dental and physiotherapy clinic.

The Clock House has seen many changes during its lifetime, but we can see it as the birthplace of two of Wycombe's most important modern buildings. From the beginnings of the art and science school came the present New Bucks University. And even though the early repertory theatre failed, its legacy was reborn in one of the towns major attractions: the Swan Theatre.

## 14. St Peter's Church, Loudwater

To many people Loudwater is a suburb of Wycombe – one passes through either on their way to the centre of town, the M40 motorway or Flackwell Heath. In fact it is still regarded as a hamlet, yet despite its modern housing and roaring traffic, it can date its origins back to the thirteenth century where it is referred to in manorial rolls as 'La Ludewatere' – no doubt a reference to the rushing River Wye.

There are few remaining old buildings in Loudwater. Loudwater House and its neighbouring half-timbered cottage on the London road are just two. However, one more building remains that reminds us that the location was once was a sleepy hamlet.

St Peter's Church was built in 1778. At that time the village would have been distant from Wycombe and surrounded by fields and woods. The church is interesting not only architecturally, but also as a good example of the changing

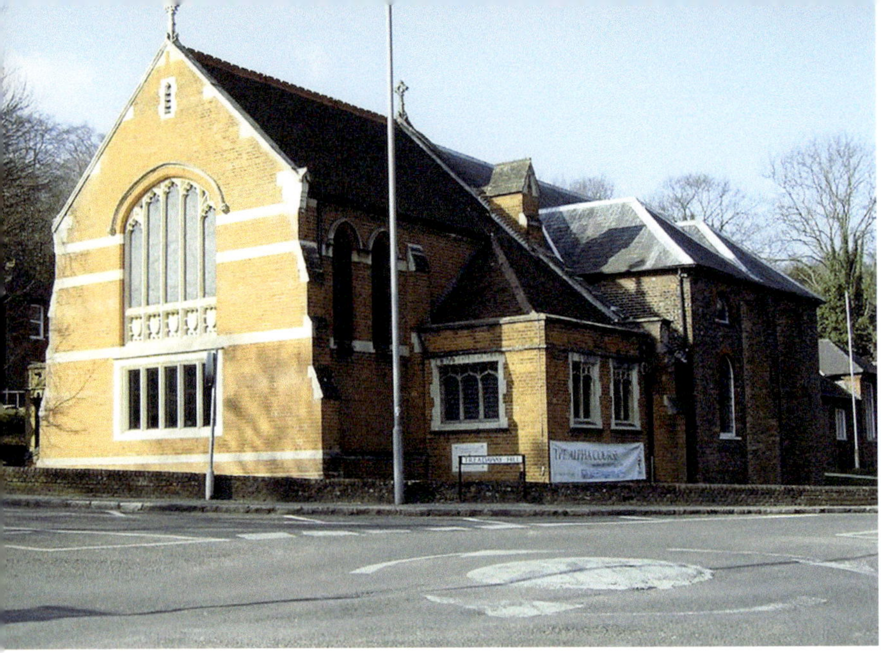

St Peter's Church, Loudwater, showings its Victorian Gothic east end.

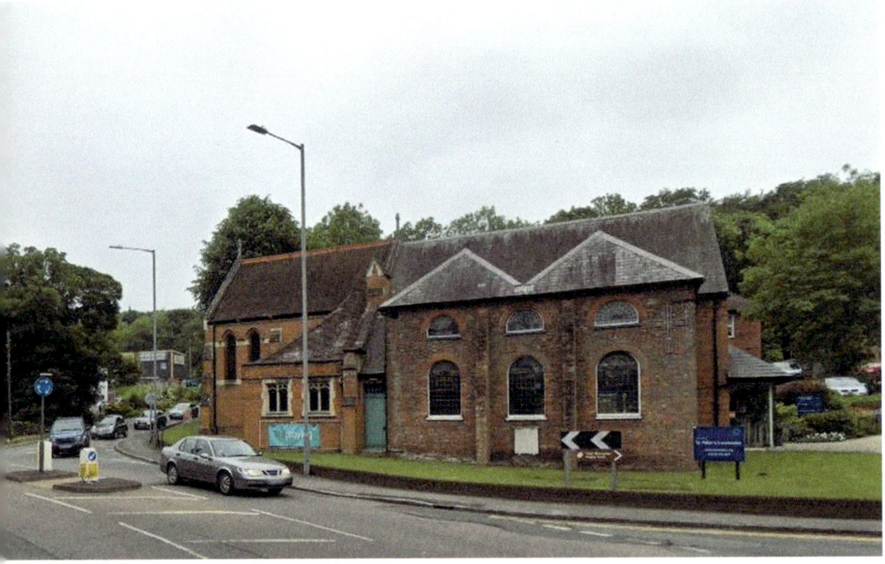

The original church with its double pyramid roof.

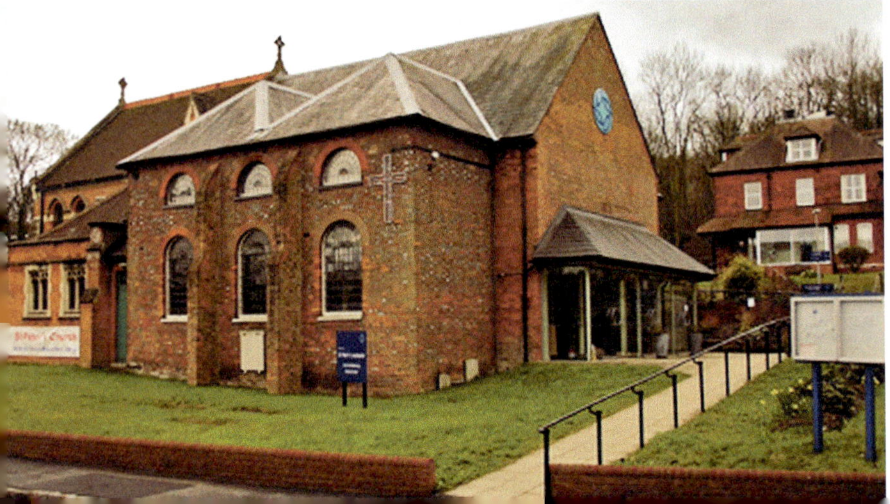

St Peter's showing its different stages of development.

fashions in church building, which stemmed historically from the Tudor and Stuart periods and leading up to the Victorian age.

St Peter's is a plain red-brick rectangular building that seems remote from the grand churches of the medieval era. Its design reflects the change in how religion was perceived and celebrated in the Georgian period. Following on from the Dissolution of the Monasteries by Henry VIII, churches in England discarded all the trappings of popish superstition. Out went the stained-glass windows, statues, painted walls and the smell of incense. In the Georgian era religion became an intellectual process of rational belief. The sermon took precedence over the sacrament, and many churches became little more that unadorned preaching boxes. St Peter's original design demonstrates this.

However, in 1840 a new view on religious service and practises developed. The Victorians were shocked at the horrors of the Industrial Revolution, which seemed to be destroying the very heart of England's green and pleasant land with grimy, smoky cities peopled by exploited workers. Their idea was to look back to an idyllic past of medieval Britain. This yearning was reflected in church design and architecture as Victorian architects built churches in the Gothic style. It didn't always work. The Gothic additions to St Peter's were added in 1903. They are perhaps a bit out of place, architecturally, as are the modern additions, to the original Georgian building. Yet they show, at least in design, the changing religious, social and architectural attitude to church buildings.

## 15. Royal Grammar School

The Royal Grammar School is more aptly described as a venerable High Wycombe institution, rather than one single building, for throughout its history it has occupied three different locations in the town. Although today its present location stands at the top of Amersham Hill, its origins go back to the sixteenth century when it was established from the lands and buildings of the dissolved Hospital of St John, the ruins of which still stand in Easton Street.

The building was converted into a school in 1550 and in 1562 was created a royal grammar school. When the school was rebuilt the remains of the eleventh-century Hospital of St John were carefully preserved within. We may view this as a curious piece of preservation by the Tudors. Following the Dissolution, England had become fiercely protestant. The retained religious structure that represented the rejected church of Rome is odd.

Nonetheless it remained the town's grammar school for the next 300 years, yet the ancient Romanesque ruins within the sixteenth-century building were lost to memory until it was rediscovered in 1840 following repairs to the master's house.

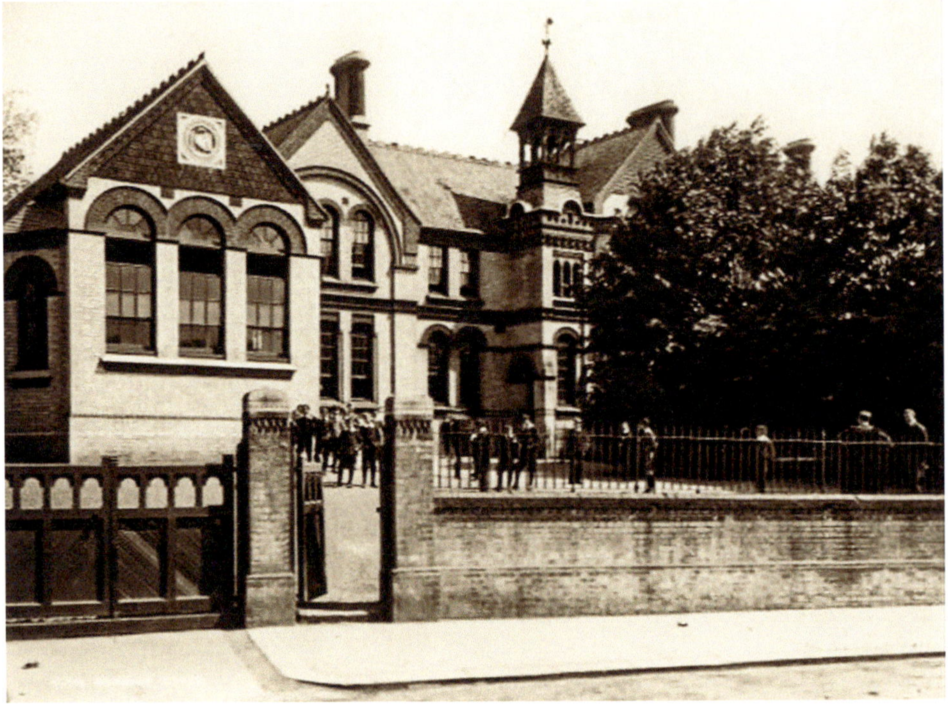

The Royal Grammar School in the late nineteenth century.

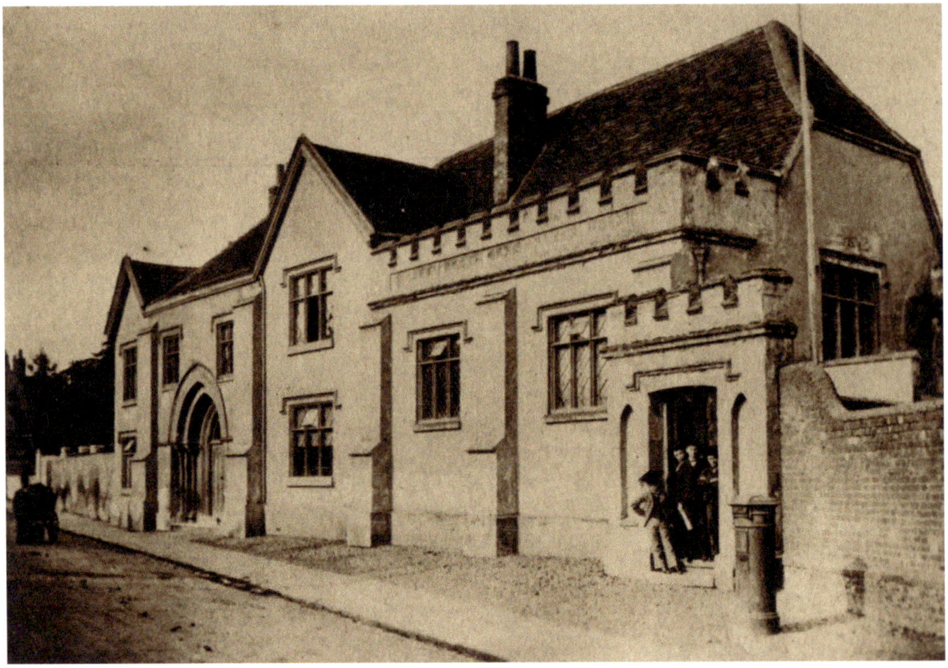

The original grammar school was adapted from the ruins of St John's Hospital.

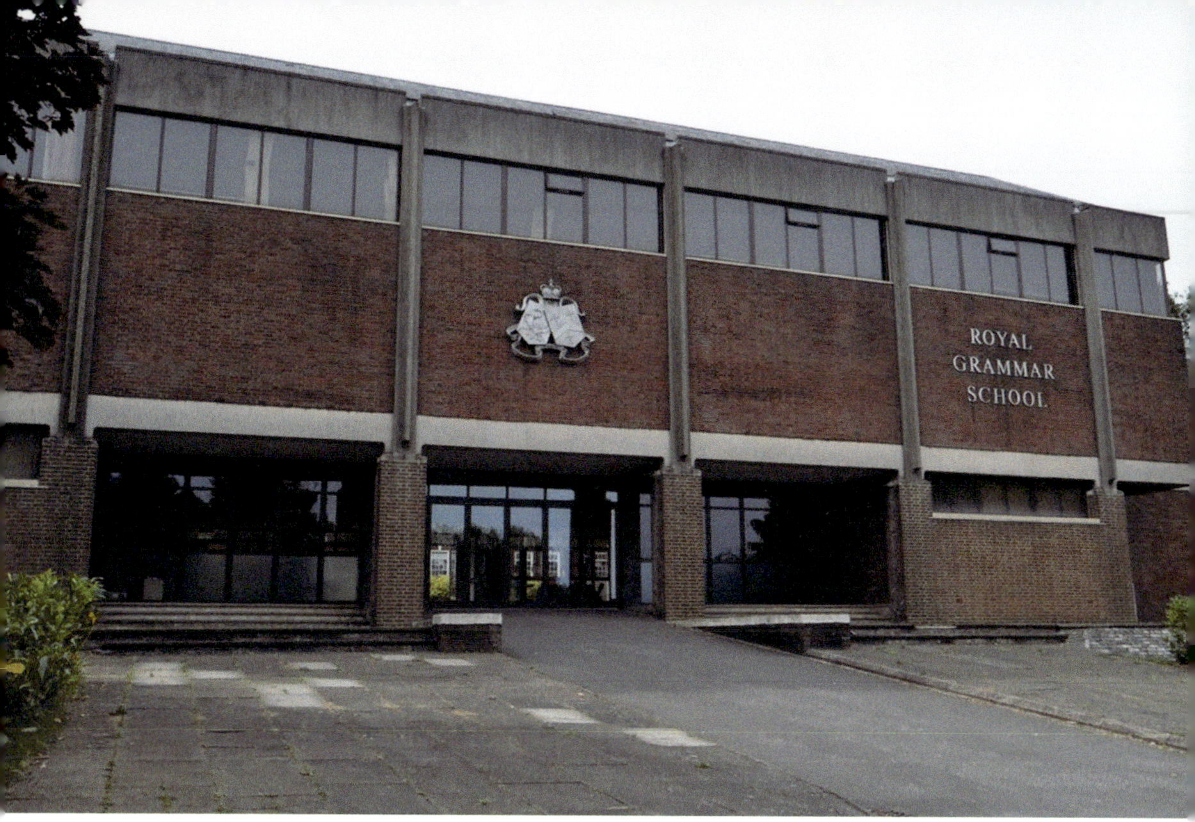


The modern frontage of today's school on Amersham Hill.

Eventually the school became too small for the growing town and increasing student numbers. In 1883 a new building was designed in the Victorian Gothic style just to the rear of the old school. Strangely, at the same time, as the Tudor buildings were demolished, the ruins of the eleventh-century hospital were once again exposed to view. We may wonder why they were not demolished. Perhaps the Victorians' love of all things medieval guaranteed their survival. The school remained in Easton Street until 1906 when they moved to their new location on Amersham Hill.

## 16. Nags Head

Sometimes the historical and cultural importance of a town's buildings is not to be found in what one might think of as the usual landmarks. Yes, Wycombe can boast its thirteenth-century church, Guildhall, eleventh-century ruins of St John's Hospital and many grand eighteenth-century houses. Yet, there are other sites, many would agree, that are just as important to the history and identity of the town as those to be found in the regular guidebooks.

The Nags Head public house was built in 1885 and was for a time the HQ of the embryonic Wycombe Wanderers FC. Like most of the town's hostelries it existed for much of its history as a normal pub, with those patrons treating it

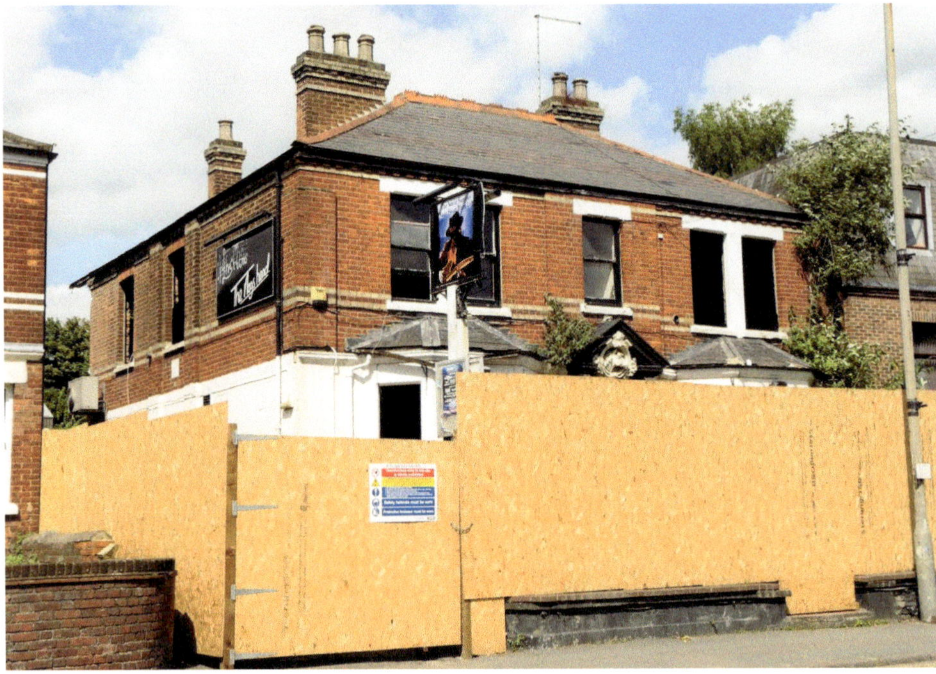

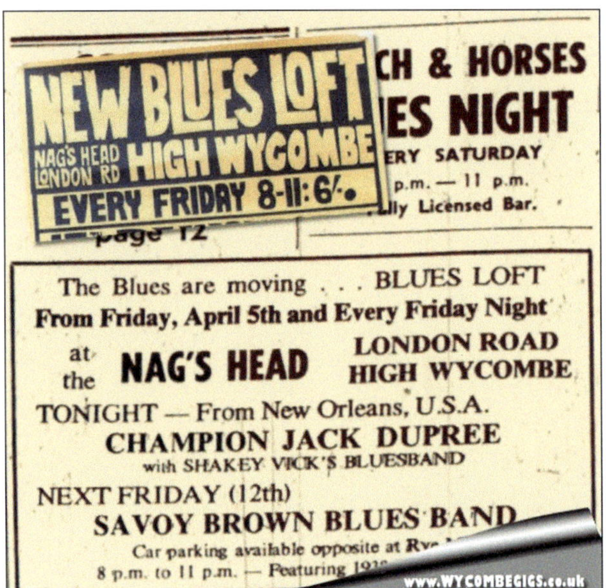


*Above*: The boarded-up frontage at the Nags Head during redevelopment.

*Left*: A poster reminding us that the great American blues men played at the Nags.

as their local. However, in the 1960s, that decade of social, cultural and artistic change, the pub became not just Wycombe's leading music venue, but one of the counties most renowned rock and blues scenes.

It was established by Ron Watts, who set up the 'Blues Loft' in a room at the back of the pub, and soon became the place to watch and listen to those bands that would go on to rock super-stardom. The early acts included legendary veteran American blues men such as Howling Wolf, Champion Jack Dupree and John Lee Hooker. There were also British acts such as Jethro Tull, Fleetwood Mac, The Police, Status Quo, Thin Lizzy and the infamous Sex Pistols.

Sadly, possibly because of changes in youth culture and popular music in general, live music ceased at the Nags Head in 1990. The pub continued under different names including The Pride, which was a meeting place for Wycombe's gay community, and The Office. Both new reincarnations were unsuccessful, and in 2005 the pub reverted back to putting on live music.

The writing, however, was on the wall for the Nags Head. It hung on until 2012, when the last tenants were evicted by the owning brewery, which sold the pub to a developer. Today the building still stands, but its interior has been converted into apartments.

## 17. Little Market House

Little Market House dates from the eighteenth century, replacing the earlier shambles built in 1627. The shambles gets its name from 'Street of Butchers', from the medieval word 'shame' or 'booth', because butchers had benches outside to display meat. For a time the market house was known as the hog market because pigs were kept at the rear. The building was rebuilt in 1771 by Scotsman Robert Adam, one of the greatest architects of the eighteenth century. He designed buildings in London, Bath and many in Scotland. It is octagonal in design, yet it is not considered one of his best. It was restored in 1807, again in 1843, and today it is affectionately known throughout Wycombe as the Pepper Pot.

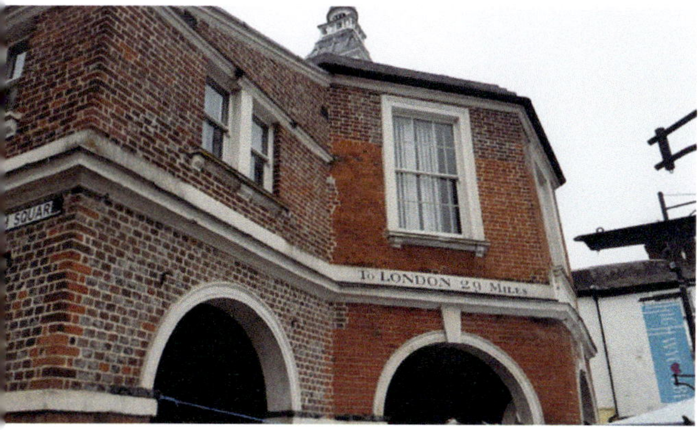


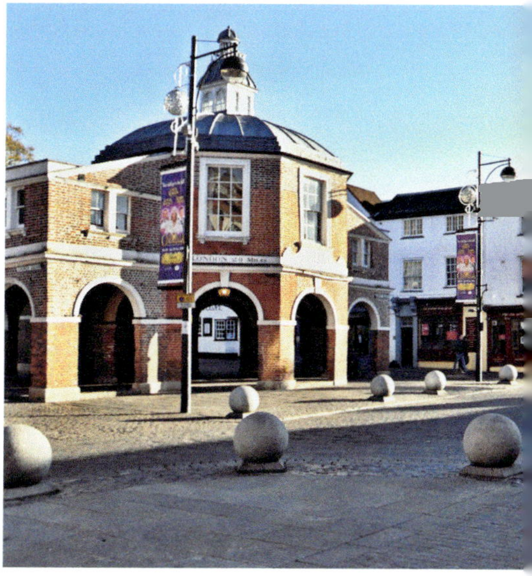

*Above*: The Pepper Pot showing the distance to London.

*Right*: The Little Market House on the high street, affectionately known as the Pepper Pot.

## 18. Castle Hill House

Castle Hill House and its surrounding grounds and gardens are one of the most interesting, and possibly confusing, locations in High Wycombe. It stands in Priory Avenue, just north of the town centre and west of the railway station. The site has been occupied from at least the eleventh century when the land was given to the nuns of Godstow Nunnery, near Oxford, by Henry II. Following the Reformation the lands were seized by Henry VIII, and seemed to have remained crown land, for in 1609 they were leased out by James I.

The house was built in possibly the late sixteenth or seventeenth century. It is a modest two-storey structure, and throughout its history has been owned by several local notable families including the Welles, Nash, Carrington and Pearce. It was added to in 1809 when the façade was remodelled in the Regency style. The gardens were originality larger and probably stretched as far as the present cutting of the railway for the land was sold to the Wycombe Railway by Lord Carrington. Today it is the home of Wycombe Museum and the house and grounds are open to the public.

Perhaps more intriguing and puzzling are the grounds themselves, for the gardens are said to contain the remains of a motte from an early Norman castle. Following the conquest of Anglo-Saxon England, the Normans constructed many motte-and-baily castles throughout the land. In ancient documents there are references to a castle at Wycombe being held by Robert de Vipont, lord of the manor during the reign of King John (1199–1216).

During the civil war between Matilda and King Stephen (1135–53) Wycombe Castle was said to have been attacked by the king. Yet some historians believe that the besieged fortress was not the one on Castle Hill but Desborough Castle, a few miles to the west (see Desborough Castle). The mound in Castle Hill Gardens is thought to be a nineteenth-century folly, which was once topped by a sham (ruin). However, in 1820, archaeologists digging at Castle Hill discovered a number of

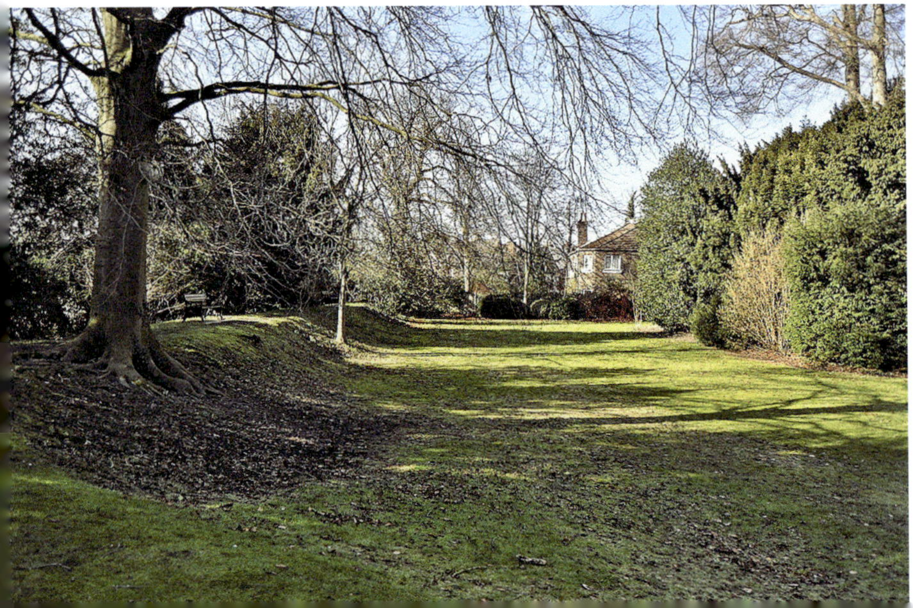

The grounds of Castle Hill House. The castle motte is situated in the trees to the right.

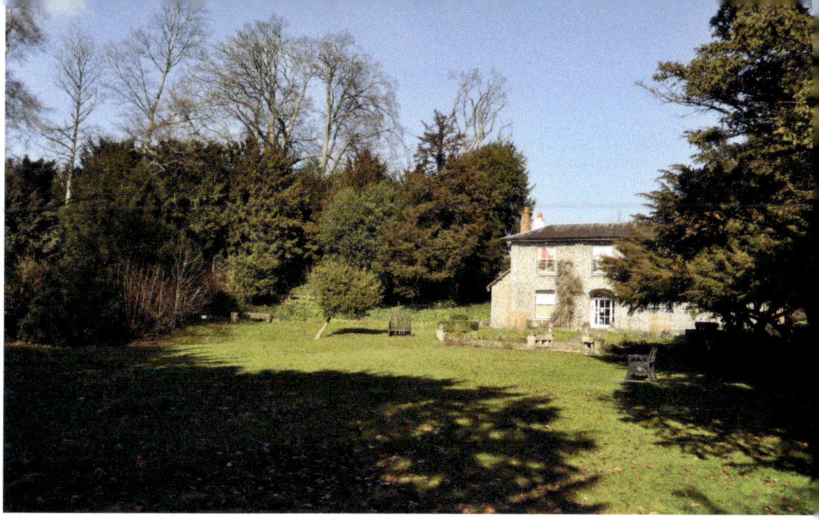
Castle Hill House.

large arrows at the base of the motte suggesting it was, at one time, the scene of fighting. The historians and archaeologists will continue to debate the site until further digging uncovers Castle Hill's secrets.

However, what is not in dispute is that the Castle Hill Gardens is the site of an Anglo-Saxon burial. It is thought to date from either the fifth or seventh century. The skeleton of a young woman unearthed from a barrow, which was situated by the entrance gates to the gardens, is thought to be the daughter of an Anglo-Saxon chieftain who had his base at Taplow, some 8 miles from Wycombe.

## 19. Magdala House, Terriers

Many people probably pass by this almost hidden house set back among the trees on Terriers Green and never give it a second thought. Some may see it on their way to catch a plane at the airport to travel to holidays oversees. Next time you pass through Terriers give a mental nod to the man whose family home was Magdala House. It was here in July 1882 that one of the leading pioneers of British aviation was born.

Sir Geoffrey de Havilland is arguably the father of international air passenger travel. He was educated at Oxford and Crystal Palace School of Engineering, initially working in motor car design and manufacture. However, from 1909 he embarked on a career of designing, building and flying aircraft, which he devoted himself to for the rest of his life.

He built his first aircraft in December 1909, making his first flight in 1910 from a field in Berkshire. In 1912 he established a new altitude record when he reached a height of over 10,000 feet. Many of de Havilland-designed planes were used in the First World War, and he was promoted to Flight Commander.

He continued to design aircraft for the war effort, and in 1941 created what is considered the best precision bomber of the Second World War: the Mosquito, nicknamed the 'wooden wonder'. It was the most versatile warplane ever built, and could carry a 3,000 lb bomb load at 270 mph at 15, 000 feet for 3,000 miles.

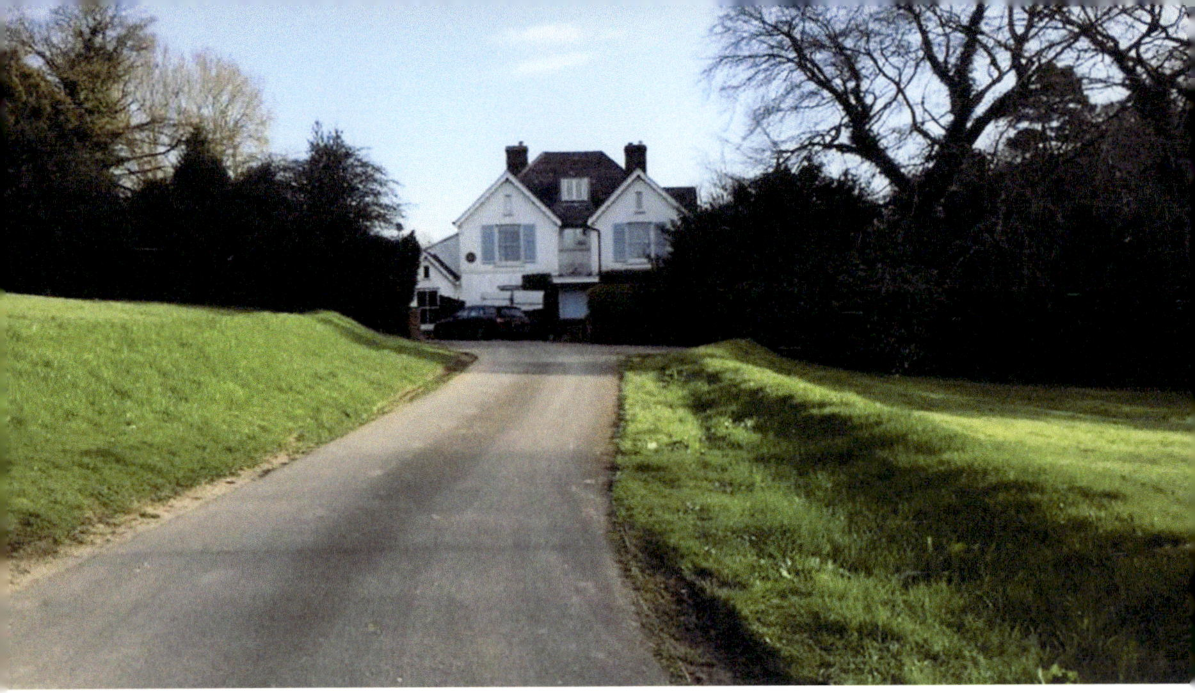

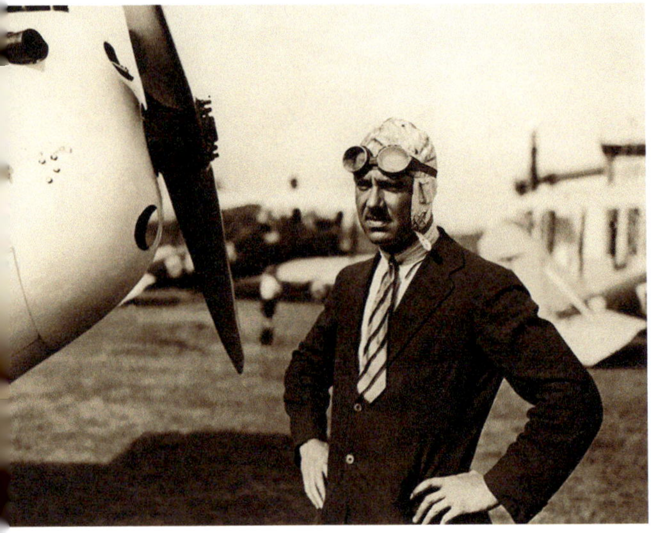

*Above*: Magdala House on Terriers Green, birthplace of Sir Geoffrey de Havilland.

*Left*: De Havilland, one of Britain's foremost aviation pioneers.

Despite the success of de Havilland's aircraft, his pioneering spirit also brought family tragedy. Two of his sons were killed in test flights, which drove his first wife to a nervous breakdown and early death.

In 1949 de Havilland developed and manufactured the world's first commercial airliner: the Comet. It was considered the Concord of its day, and opened up the world to what would become mass tourism.

Geoffrey de Havilland died in May 1965, aged eighty-two, and is recognised the world over as a giant in the field of military and commercial aviation. His family tree sprouted many branches, as his cousins were the Hollywood actresses Oliver de Havilland and Joan Fontaine.

## 20. St Francis' Church, Terriers

The area of Terriers, around a mile and a half outside the centre of Wycombe, is a curious location. The name isn't mentioned in documents until 1714, and either relates to the name of a family which farmed the area, or derives from people 'tarrying' in the locale before moving on after leaving Wycombe. The absence of any documentary evidence suggests that Terriers may have been part of Kings Wood, a medieval hunting forest. The area was still relatively rural and sparsely populated in the 1930s, which poses the question as to why a grand substantial church was built there.

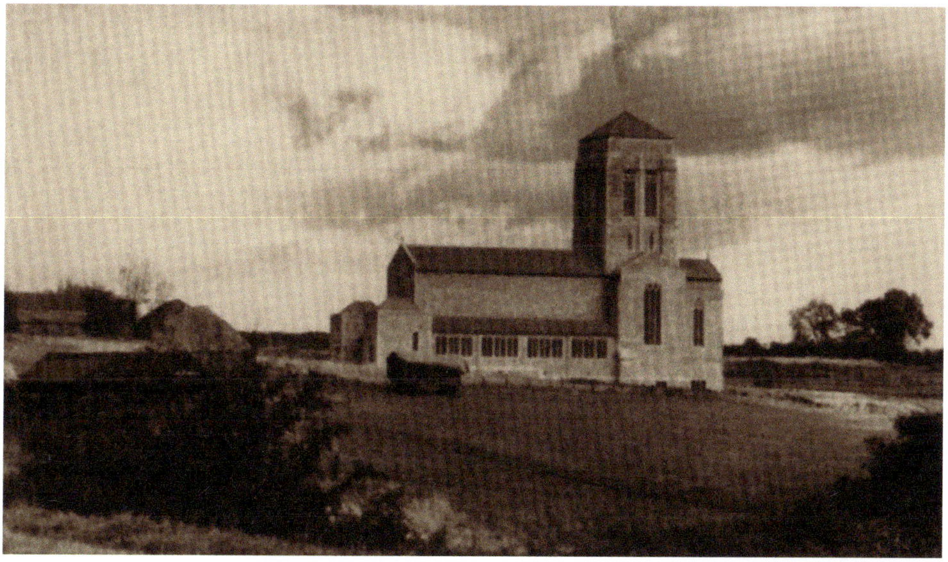

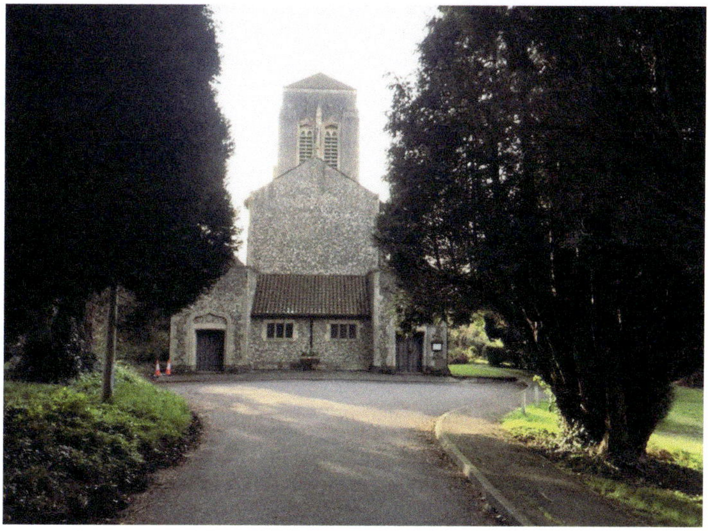

*Above*: St Francis' Church was designed by Sir Giles Gilbert Scott.

*Right*: The church in the 1930s just after construction.

The Church of St Francis of Assisi was built in 1930 from designs by Sir Giles Gilbert Scott, one of the most eminent architects of the twentieth century. His buildings include Liverpool Cathedral and Battersea Power Station. He is also famous for designing Britain's iconic red telephone boxes.

The church is an example of modern Gothic, and despite being considered one of Scott's finest designs, it is to some degree an impressive but austere building. It has a lofty tower and what has been described as a severe chancel, transepts and a blank nave without a clerestory.

## 21. Wheatsheaf Inn

I sometimes find it astonishing that in an ever-changing town such as Wycombe where, in the last fifteen years, the whole of its western side, along Oxford Street, has been changed beyond recognition with new buildings and development, an unassuming house situated on the high street has managed to survive almost unchanged for the last 500 years.

The Wheatsheaf Inn has, for many years, confounded historians as to its true age. Even the great architectural historian Sir Nikolaus Pevsner believed it dated to only the sixteenth century. However, in recent years research by dendrochronology (the science of dating the timbers of a building by reference to the rings on the tree stem) has proved that the wood used to construct the Wheatsheaf was felled in 1390. Therefore it is entirely possible that the inn was standing in Wycombe High Street in the year 1400.

Given such a date, it is no wonder that the early history of the pub is unclear. That it was an inn by the seventeenth century is in no doubt. The first publican that can be named with certainty is Thomas Butterfield. During the upheaval caused by the English Civil War no currency was minted, so many of Wycombe publicans and tradesmen minted their own coinage to be used in their own businesses. Butterfield issued his own tokens to be spent at the Wheatsheaf.

During the eighteenth century many of the half-timbered buildings in the high street were fronted with fashionable Georgian façades. However, the frontage of the Wheatsheaf retained its original appearance with its distinctive over hanging, jettied upper floors. In 1772 the inn was owned by Anne Squire. Her brother, Daniel, was a brewer and also Mayor of Wycombe.

By the early 1800s the Wheatsheaf became one of a number of pubs and inns in the town owned by Wheeler's Brewery. The Wheeler family were affluent bankers, and one, Thomas, served several terms as mayor.

In 1903, owing to the glut of pubs in the high Street, the Wheatsheaf was due to close. However, on the night of 1 July the inn caught fire. Miraculously it was saved from total destruction and soon after sold for £865 to Mr William Butler, who converted the property into pharmacy. In 1930 the shop once again changed hands and was converted into two shops: a tobacconists and a dry cleaners.

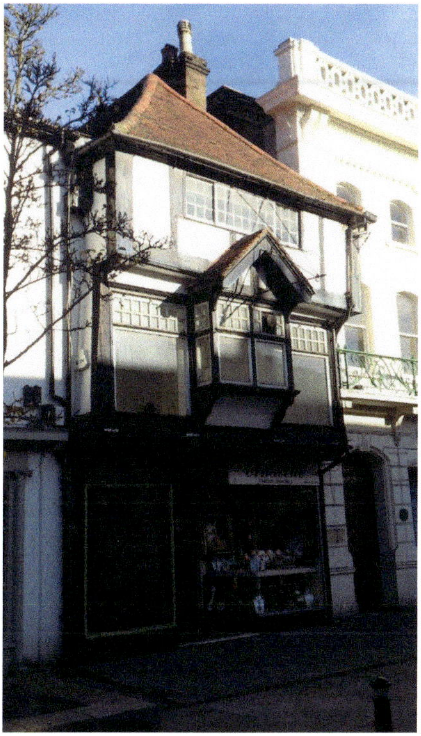

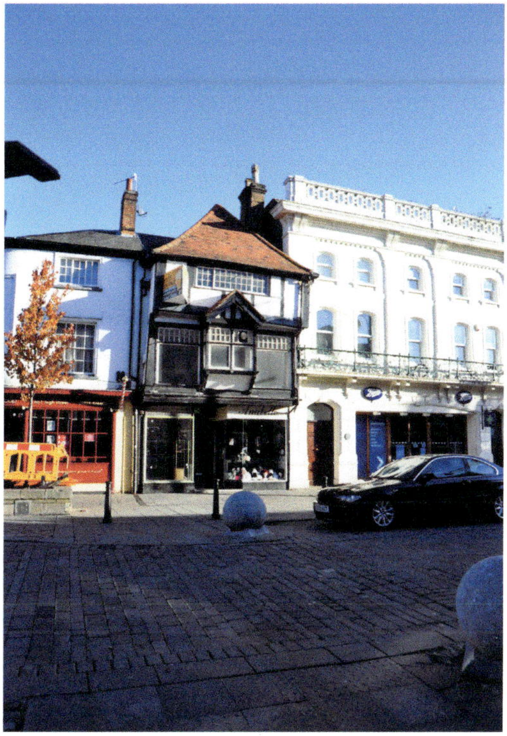

*Above left*: The Wheatsheaf Inn, the oldest secular building in Wycombe.

*Above right*: It is a miracle that the inn has survived for 500 years.

Over 500 years the old Wheatsheaf has seen a lot of history. When it was first built, the King of England was Henry IV, who had usurped the throne from his cousin Richard II. It was standing when the English defeated the French at Agincourt. When Henry VIII lopped off the heads of his two adulterous wives, their fate was probably discussed over a pint by Wheatsheaf regulars. During the English Civil War Roundhead troops would have entered its doors for a quick jar before marching off to battle. So next time you pass this ancient building take time to stop and take in its past.

## 22. Red Lion Hotel

The Red Lion Inn, which would become the Red Lion Hotel, is one of Wycombe's most celebrated buildings. It is the site of one of Wycombe's earliest coaching inns with its origins being traced back to the early thirteenth century when it was owned by the Cox family. In 1518 the family gave the inn to Brasenose College, Oxford.

The hotel was rebuilt in the early eighteenth century, but remodelled in 1772 and 1847, with an east section added in 1930. The Red Lion was the focal point

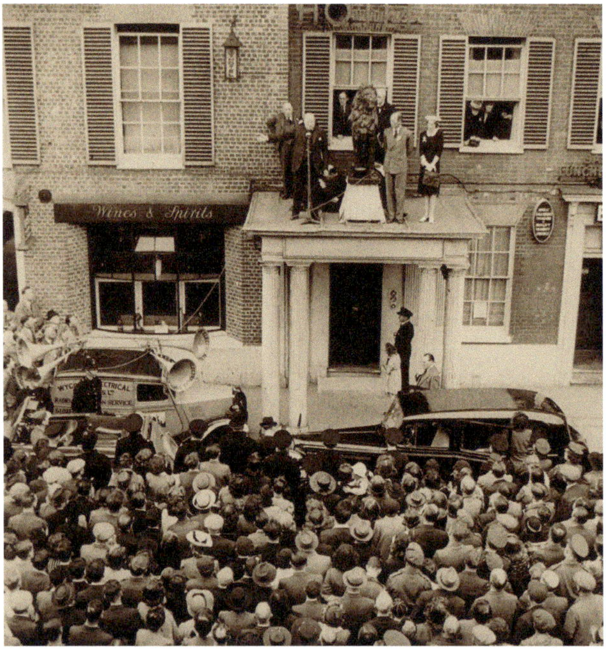

*Left*: Sir Winston Churchill addresses a crowd from the the Red Lion Hotel portico in 1946.

*Below*: The Red Lion today.

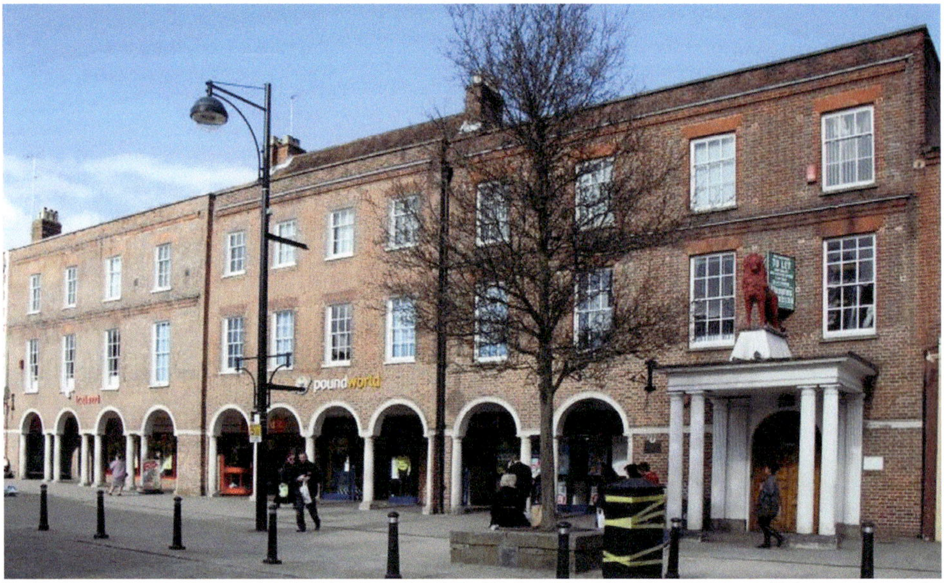

for much of the social and political life of High Wycombe. It contained the Wellington Room, a plush and sumptuous dining room that was the venue for special events and meetings of the town's clubs and societies.

Perhaps more famous and iconic than the hotel itself is its portico and the statue of a proud red lion that adorns it today. It was from this portico that Victorian statesman Benjamin Disraeli made his first political speech in 1832. Over

100 years later, in 1946, fellow Conservative politician Sir Winston Churchill also spoke from the portico.

Given such a famous and historic location it is puzzling that in 1972 the hotel was chosen as the site for the new Woolworths store. The building was altered and the portico and lion moved further to the right to accommodate the store entrance. Today Woolworths has gone, replaced with the Iceland and Poundland stores. One wonders what Disraeli and Churchill would have thought.

## 23. Rupert Gates

Perhaps nothing better illustrates the breaking down of class barriers in Britain and the retreat of the wealthy, titled gentry than the shrinkage of the vast estates of the once landowning families. In Wycombe, one can see this if we ever take a leisurely stroll across Hughenden Park. Now open to all, it was once the land of Victorian statesman Benjamin Disraeli where trespassers in the late nineteenth century would have been soon seen off by bailiffs with shotguns.

Similarly, if a resident of Victorian Wycombe made his way along the high street, he would know that the grand Gothic gates, which stood opposite Crendon Lane, were the entrance to Wycombe Abbey. Not a religious establishment but the home of the Carrington family, wealthy Buckinghamshire landowners.

The gates were so named after a Carrington family member, and were built in a cod, castellated Gothic with crenelated battlements. A suitable entrance to one of Wycombe great houses. The gates led into a woodland drive, across a tiny lake and on to the abbey, which was surrounded by grounds that looked up to the Beech-covered hills. The building was situated less than half a mile from Wycombe High Street, but might well have been in another remote leafy county.

In 1896 the Carringtons sold the abbey and part of the grounds to the girls' education company which became Wycombe Abbey School, and five years later moved into Dawes Hill House, a modest farmhouse within the grounds, and converted it into a mansion. The drive, which had led from the gates, was given

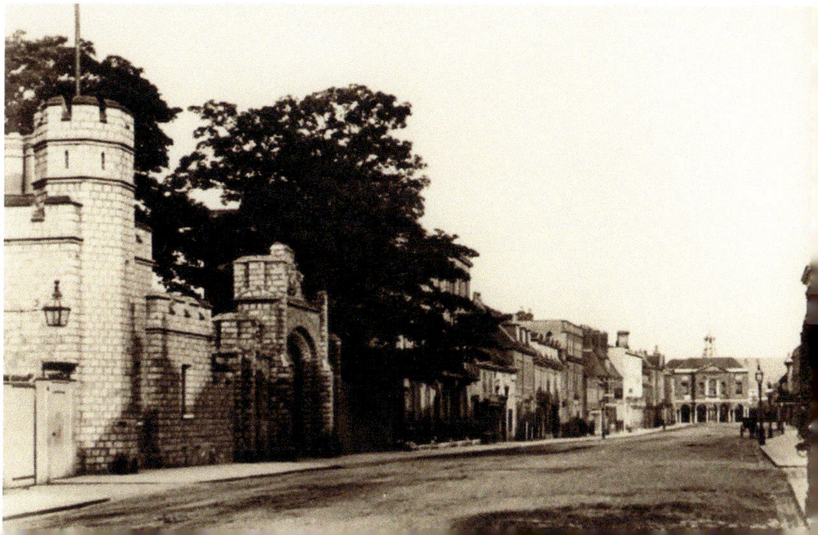

The Rupert Gates in their original position on the high street.

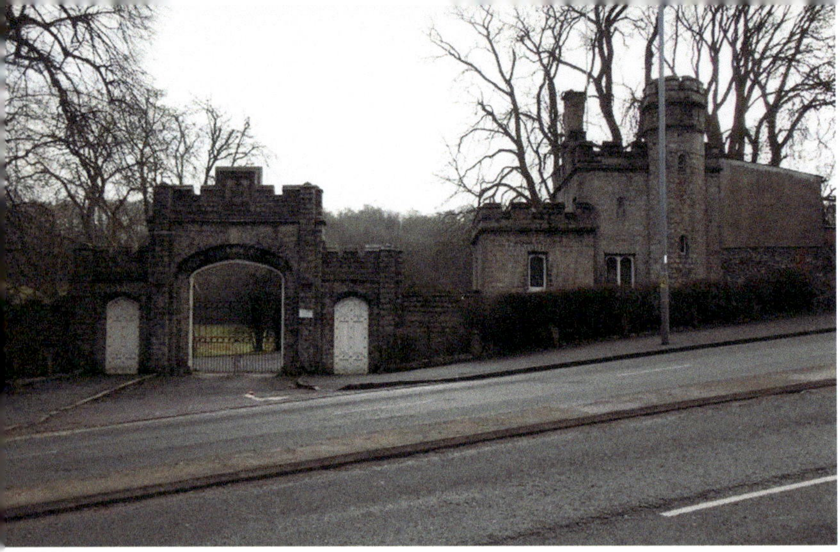

The Rupert Gates on Marlow Hill.

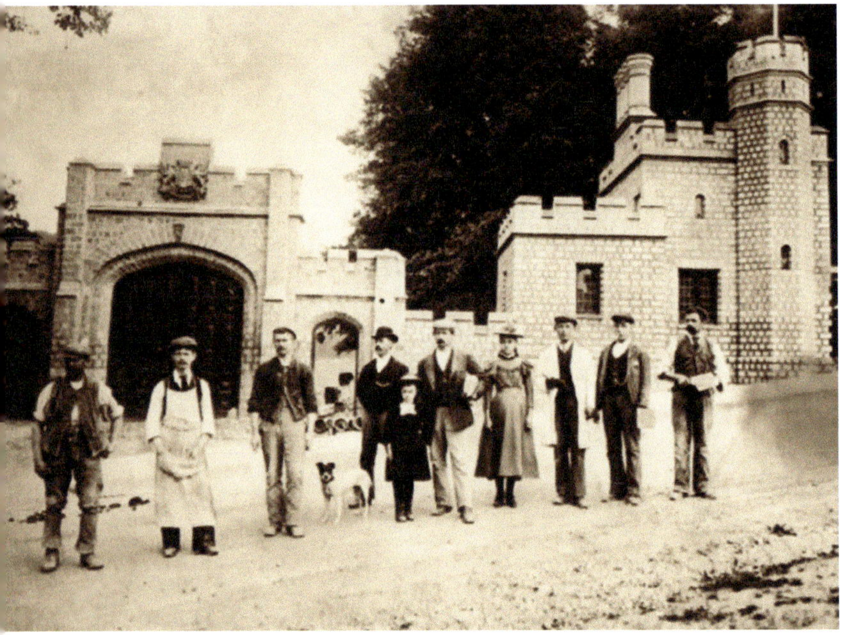

Estate workers stand outside the gates soon after their relocation.

back to the town for the erection of a new town hall and other public buildings. It was named Queen Victoria Road in memory of Queen Victoria.

The gates were no longer needed yet, incredibly, they were not demolished, but dismantled and re-erected halfway up Marlow Hill to create a new entrance to the Carringtons' new house. They still stand today.

## 24. Town Hall, Queen Victoria Road

Prior to a new town hall being built in Wycombe, the town's administration was carried out at the guildhall. Lord Carrington originally offered a site in Castle

Street for the new council building; this, however, was rejected and following the removal of the Rupert Gates in the high Street, the land which was the driveway to Wycombe Abbey was developed into a road and named after Queen Victoria. It was in fact being given back to the town before the building of the abbey and its extensive grounds. This was Horsenden Lane. It was practically on the outskirts of Wycombe, and it was here in 1643 that barricades were erected and the townsfolk beat off an attack by the Royalists during the Civil War.

The first building to be constructed in Queen Victoria Road was the town hall in 1904. It contains a main hall with seating for over 1,000 people. There was also a stage, dressing rooms, gallery and organ. The room above the entrance hall gained the name the Red Room due to its coloured hangings. The room also contains five stained-glass windows depicting the educational and commercial history of the town. There are portraits of Buckinghamshire worthies: Hampden, Burke, Disraeli and William Penn.

The Red Room was later panelled in oak and has become known as the Oak Room. The building was restored in 1972 to cater for more entertainment needs when the gallery was transformed into a lounge bar. Indeed, apart from its function as the town's administrator, the building has also seen some performances from many of Britain's pop and rock groups before they went on to international fame. The Who, Pink Floyd, the Rolling Stones and Jethro Tull all trod the boards at the town hall.

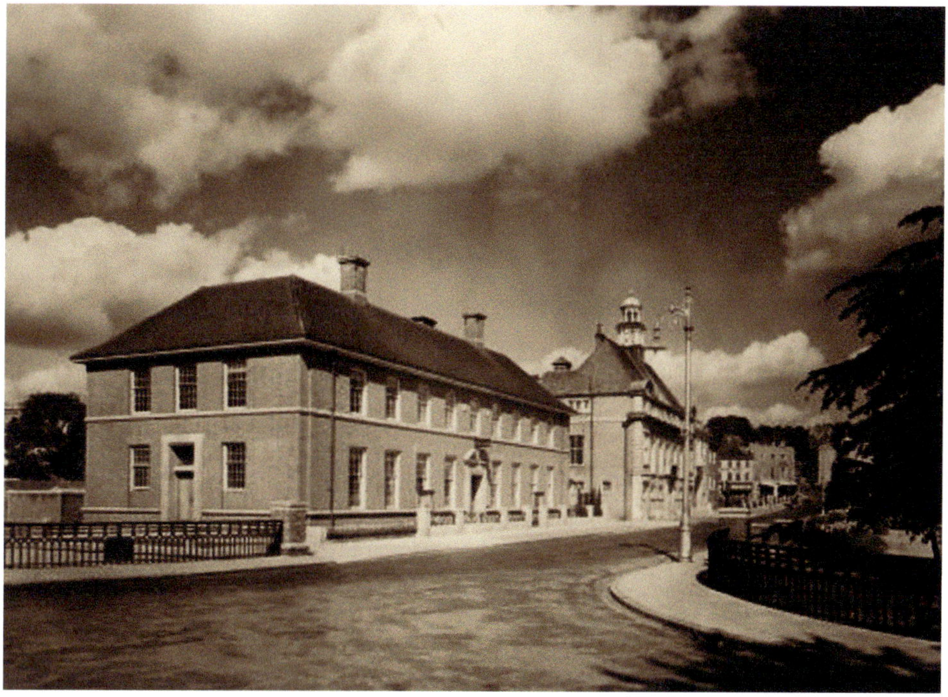

The Town Hall and Wycombe police station soon after their construction in the 1930s.

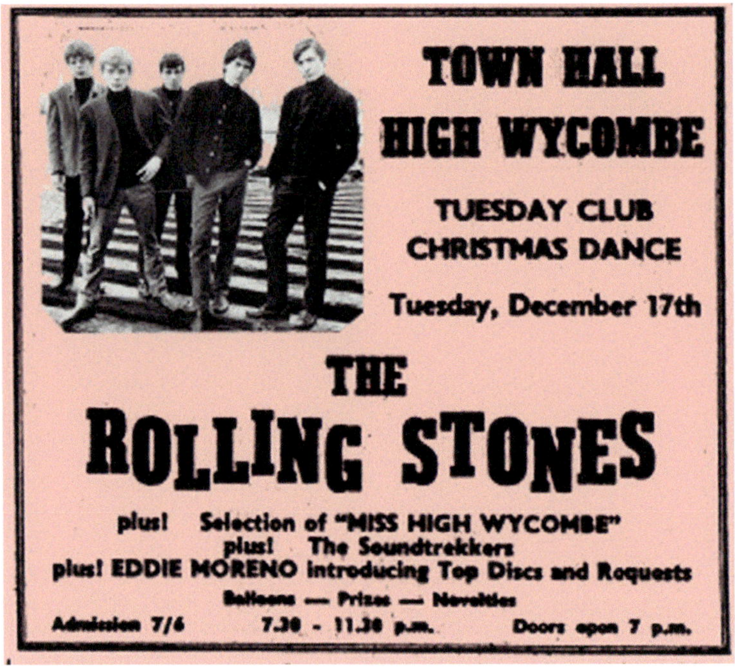


Many of Britain's rock groups started their careers playing venues like the Town Hall.

## 25. Union Baptist Chapel

The modern Baptist Church trace their history back to the seventeenth and eighteenth centuries when they separated from the Church of England following the Act of Uniformity in 1662 where many people were dissatisfied with the achievements of the Protestant Reformation. South Buckinghamshire has a long tradition of Nonconformism, including Baptists, and throughout Wycombe one can find many Baptist churches and chapels.

The Union Baptist Chapel in Easton Street was originality built in 1845. Like today, it stands back from the street and can easily be missed. Despite the Baptists' Protestant beliefs, the chapel was built in a rather sumptuous, classical style and is curious in design for its date as most Victorians preferred their churches to be constructed in the Gothic manner. Yet it seems that the Baptists long held a tradition for their chapels to be built in such a grand way.

Sadly, the chapel burnt down in a spectacular fire in 1905. It was quickly rebuilt in a more flamboyant classical style with an Italianate façade. It still stands as one of Wycombe's most handsome buildings.

The Baptists were not always to everyone's taste. During their worship at the chapel local barrister John Stone hired a man to march up and down his garden beating a drum to disturb the worshippers. Today, happily, the brethren can worship in relative peace.

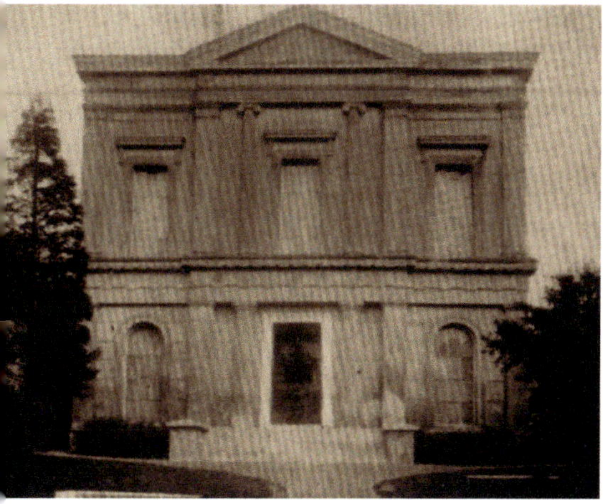

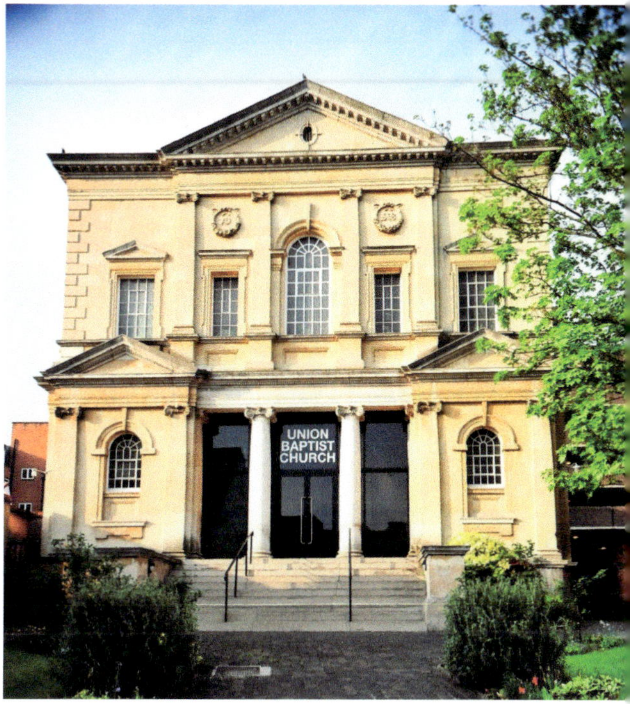


*Above*: The first Union Baptist Chapel before it was destroyed by fire in 1905.

*Right*: The classical façade of the rebuilt chapel.

## 26. Wycombe Swan Theatre

Three buildings represent the regeneration of Wycombe over the last twenty-five years: one is the Eden Shopping Centre, the second is the rejuvenated New Bucks University, and the third is the Wycombe Swan Theatre. Curiously, two have their origins in the Clock House on Frogmore. It was here that the foundations for the university were laid with the opening of the School for Science and Art in 1893. It was also here that Wycombe's first repertory theatre was established in 1946. Sadly the theatre failed, but not the idea of bringing the stage to Wycombe.

The Swan was opened in 1992 and has become one of Britain's leading regional theatres. It is a strikingly designed building, and comprises a main theatre, Wycombe Swan Town Hall and the Oak Room. It is home to the Swan Youth Theatre, a permanent Youth Theatre Company open to ten to nineteen-year-olds, which organise workshops and performance-based activities.

Strangely for a building so recently built it is said to be haunted. Staff have often reported seeing the figure of a man sitting in one of the seats of the auditorium after the performance has finished. When they approach the figure to tell him that the show has ended and they were locking up for the night, the person is nowhere to be seen.

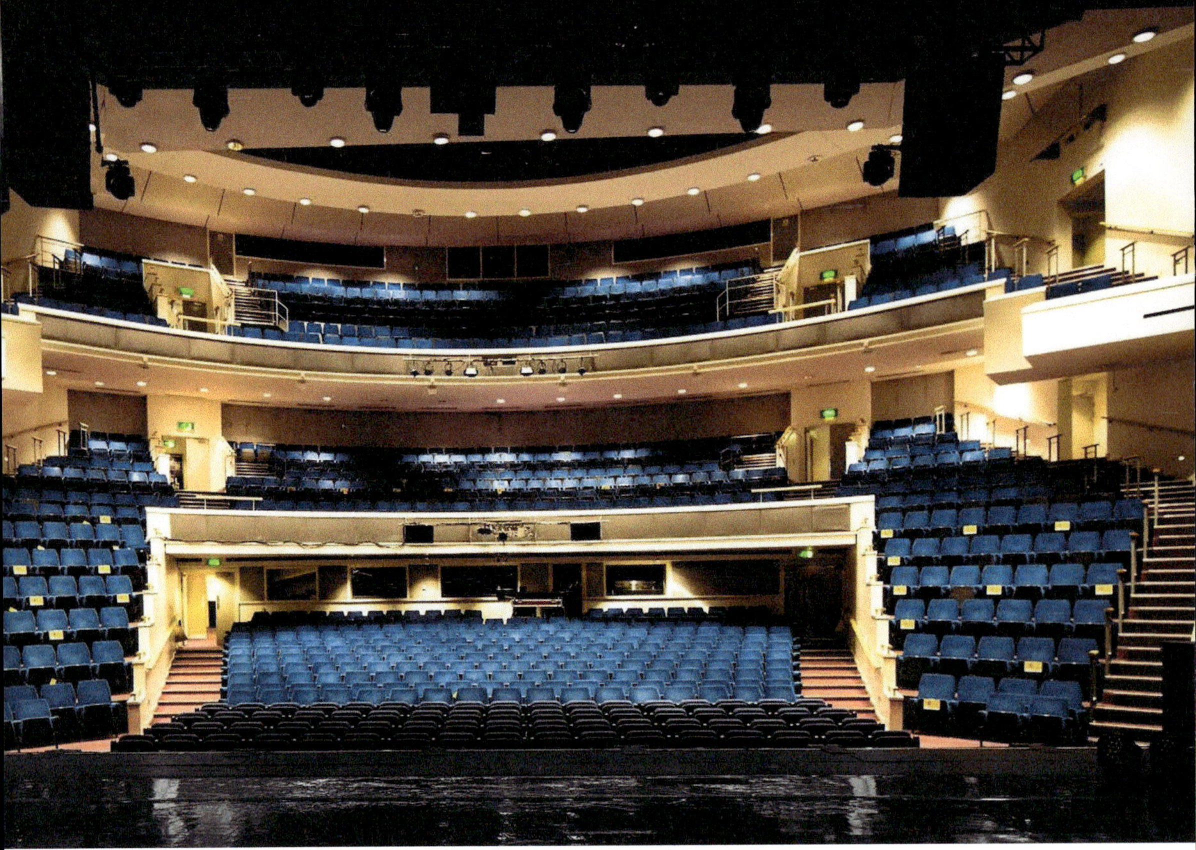

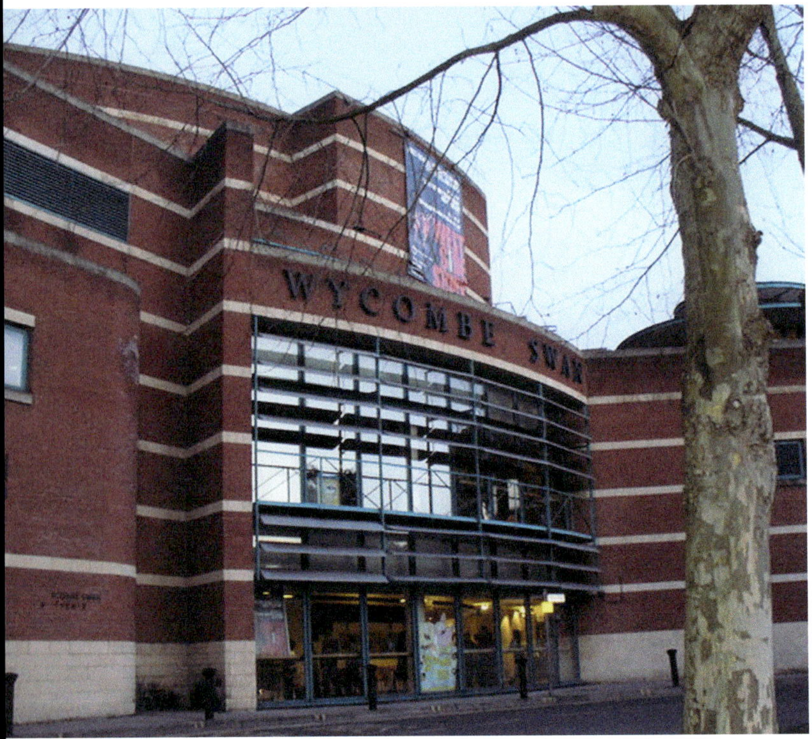


*Above*: The grand auditorium of the Swan Theatre.

*Left*: The front of the Swan Theatre, one of Wycombe's most striking buildings.

## 27. Pann Mill

'The river made the mills, the mills made the market and the market made the town.' So said John Parker, High Wycombe town clerk in 1878. There has been a mill on the Pann Mill site since the eleventh century where it is mentioned in the Domesday Book. It takes its names from one Roger de Panil, a knight during the reign of Henry II (1154–1189). The king had given de Panil the mill, and considerable land went with it for his service in the crusades.

There is a long history of mills operating on the River Wye, which flows for some 10 miles from its source by West Wycombe to Bourne End. The drop of the river by some 200 feet along its course powered up to thirty mills. Although some of the mills milled corn, their main business was paper making, and it is recorded by 1816 that more than 150 men were employed in the mills along the Wye Valley. However, the introduction, in 1830, of the Fourdrinier machine, which produces a continuous roll of paper, put many men out of work. Their redundancy led to unrest and riots in which the machines were smashed. The authorities were severe in their treatment of the rioters, and twenty men were punished by penal transportation to Tasmania.

Pann Mill has seen many changes throughout its history. The Georgian mill was substantially altered in the late nineteenth century and again in the early twentieth. Incredibly, for a building that is so connected with the history and development of Wycombe, it was mostly demolished in 1971. If it were not for the valiant efforts of

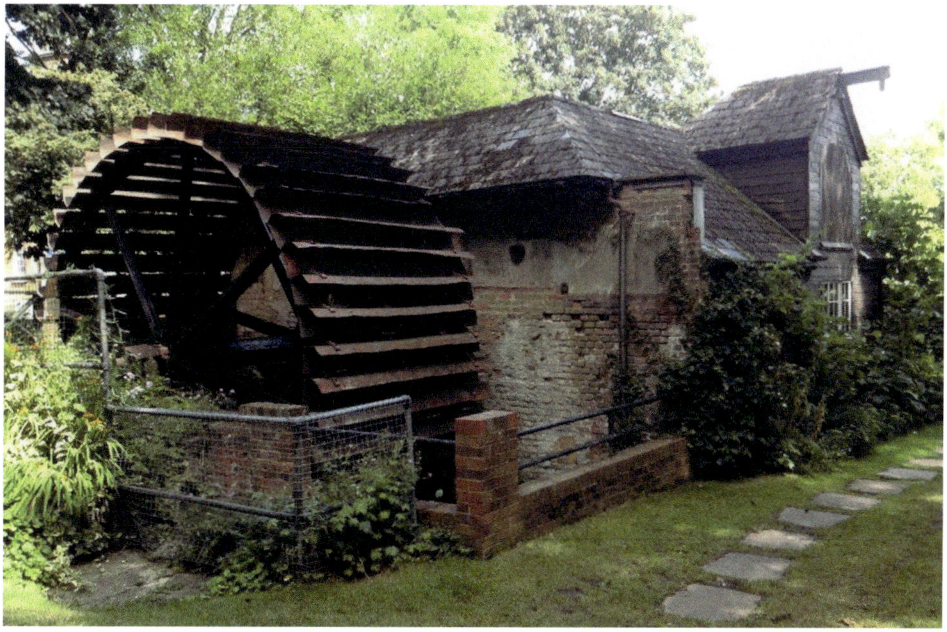

Pann Mill on the River Wye, which has been lovingly restored and cared for by the Wycombe Historical Society.

the High Wycombe society, who saved the remains of the site and restored the mill and its cast-iron waterwheel, part of the towns past would have been lost forever.

Pann Mill is the only remaining mill on the River Wye. It is arguable that had it not existed, along with the other mills that worked the river, High Wycombe might not have developed and may well have remained an insignificant Chiltern backwater.

## 28. West Wycombe Hill Fort

The idea that High Wycombe is an archetypal modern home counties town and a satellite of London is often a view expressed by many who know little of Wycombe's history and initially discover it by way of its 1930s suburban housing estates that dot and crowd the town's surrounding hills. It would be a wrong impression, for just over a mile from the town centre stands an ancient structure erected centuries before the Romans set foot in Britain.

West Wycombe hill fort was constructed between the fourth and fifth century BC, possibly by the Catuvellauni people. The Catuvellauni were one of a number of Celtic tribes who occupied southern Britain, including what would become Buckinghamshire, during what we now refer to as the Iron Age. It was an era that lasted from around 800 BC to the coming of the Roman legions in AD 43.

It is unknown for what purpose West Wycombe hill fort was built. It is circular and covers an area of just over a hectare and has a diameter of 120 metres. In places it is enclosed by a ditch and two massive defensive ramparts, which would have been topped by a wooden palisade, and sits imposingly 80 metres above the valley floor at the apex of the Wye Valley and the vale of Aylesbury. Such a grand position commanded, as it does today, impressive views over the surrounding grand sweep and roll of the Chiltern Hills, and would have been highly visible to anyone – foe or friend – passing along the valley below.

Although some hilltop enclosures were used for keeping livestock, the hill at West Wycombe with its steep southern and western slopes suggests that it was constructed for defensive purposes.

However, the real purpose for the construction of the hill fort may well have been for a more peaceful and spiritual nature. Although a defended settlement providing a home and security for a number of Iron Age families, the hill may well have become a local centre for trade and, more significantly, religion.

Archaeological evidence suggests that a Bronze Age pagan temple once existed on the hill, and that the Romans also built their own religious place of worship there. When the Anglo-Saxons arrived in Britain in AD 410, they brought with them their own pagan beliefs and rituals. They occupied West Wycombe Hill, or Haeferingdune as it was known to them, the hill of Haefas' people. The village, sitting just north of the hill fort ramparts, would eventually become known as Haveringdon. It was wiped out during the Black Death in the fourteenth century. Yet it is possible that

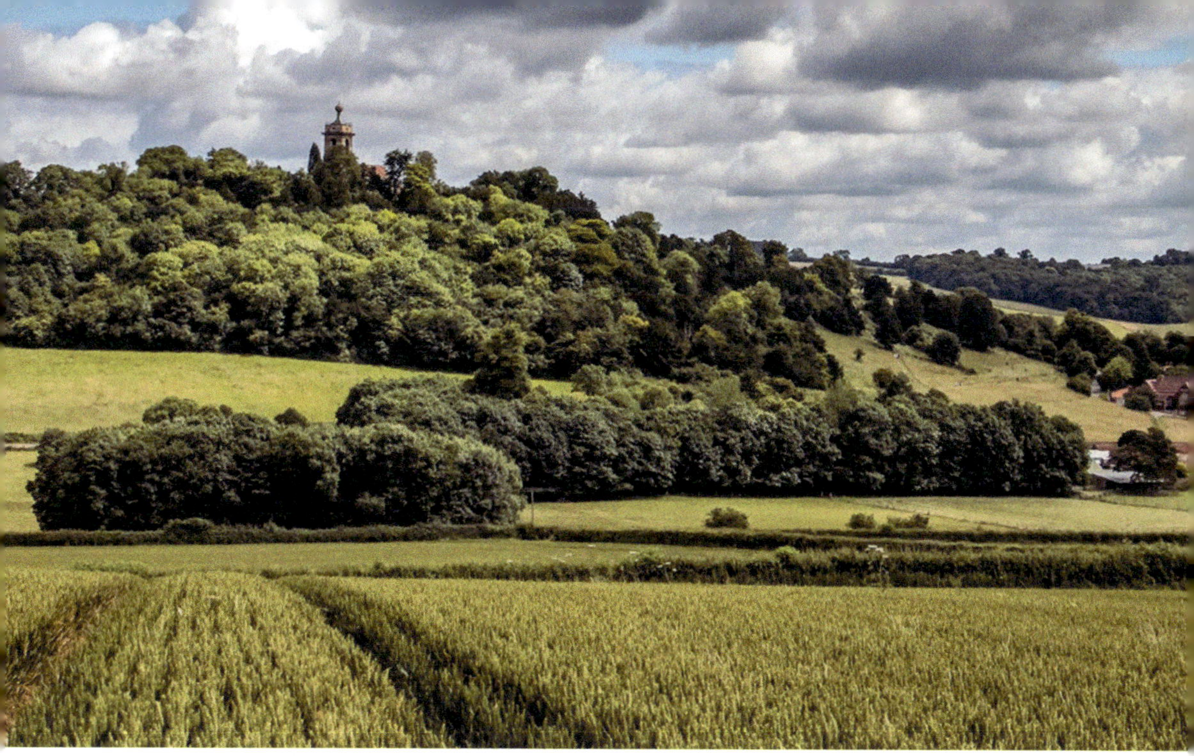

*Above*: St Lawrence's Church sits on top of the Iron Age West Wycombe hill fort.

*Below*: The view from the top of the fort looking back towards High Wycombe.

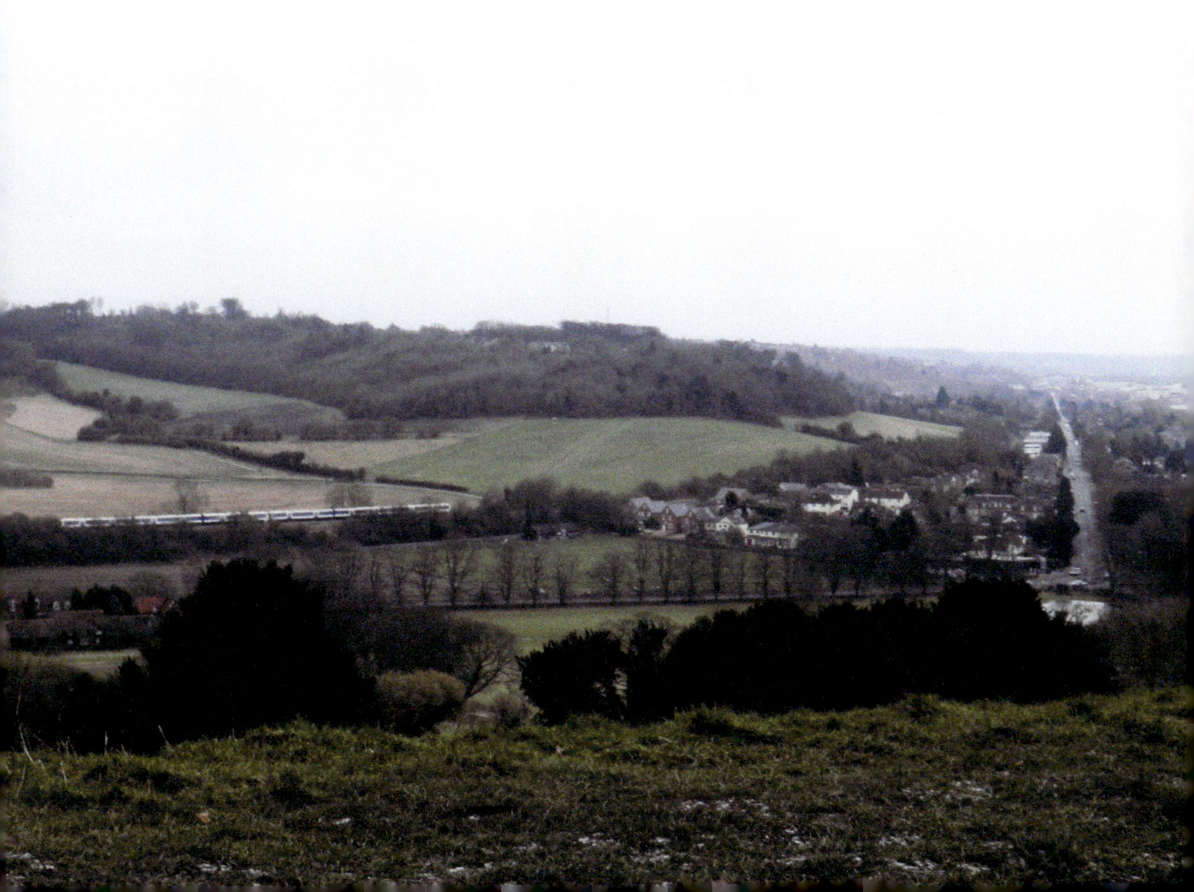

the present Church of St Lawrence, which sits at the top of the hill, stands on an earlier place of Saxon worship – the village church of Haveringdon. When the pagan Saxons were converted to Christianity in the sixth century by St Augustine his remit from the pope was to use existing pagan places of religion and incorporate Christian belief and practises within them. It seems possible that the hill has been a venerated site and place of worship from at least the fifth century BC. The present Church of St Lawrence carries on that ancient tradition.

## 29. West Wycombe Mausoleum

The most spectacular of Dashwood's ideas for West Wycombe Hill is, undoubtedly, the mausoleum he had constructed in 1765. It is an extraordinary monument to one man's vanity and the memory of his family, and, from its lofty position, can be seen for many miles around.

In 1762, George Bubb Doddington, 1st Baron Melcombe, a close friend of Dashwoods, and also a member of the Hell Fire Club, died and bequeathed to Sir Francis the sum £500, 'To build a temple to his family seat'. The lord of the manor duly set to work and engaged architect Nicholas Revett to construct a mausoleum based on the arch of Constantine in Rome.

The impressive Dashwood Mausoleum on West Wycombe Hill.

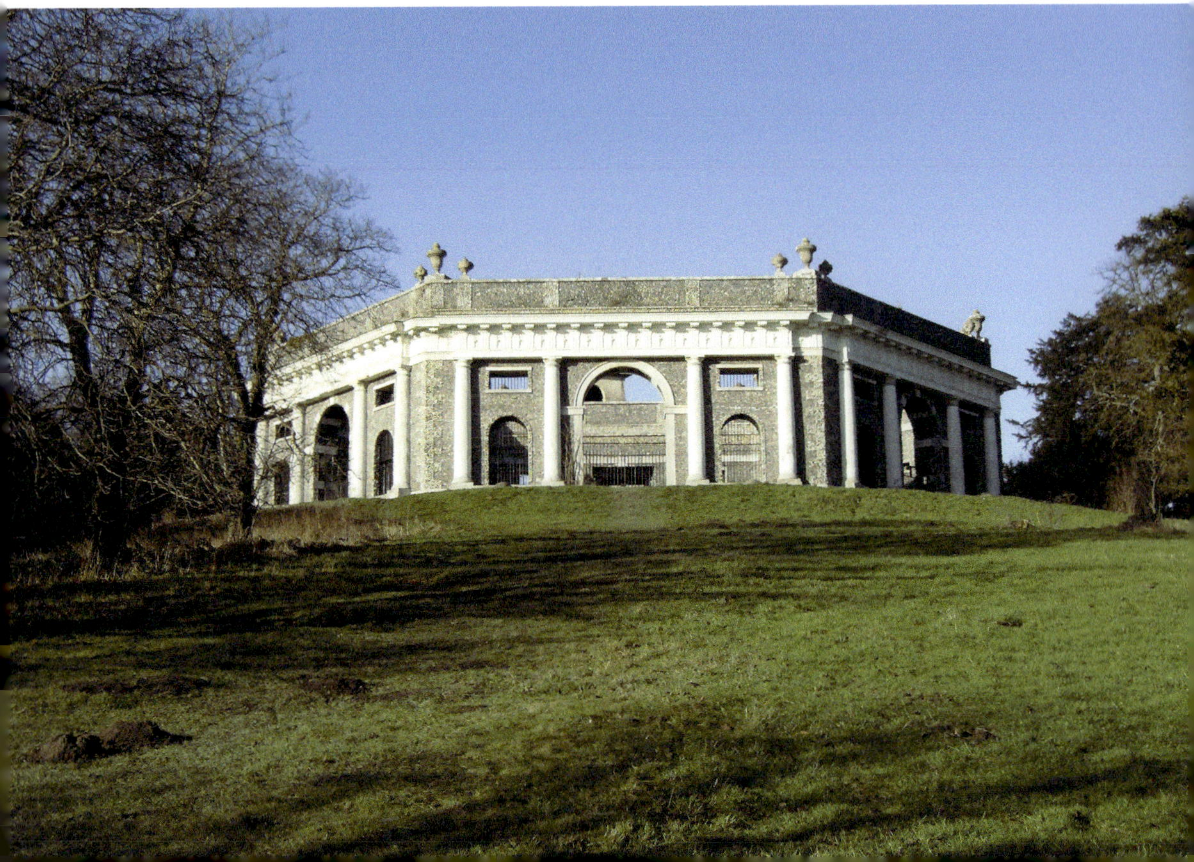

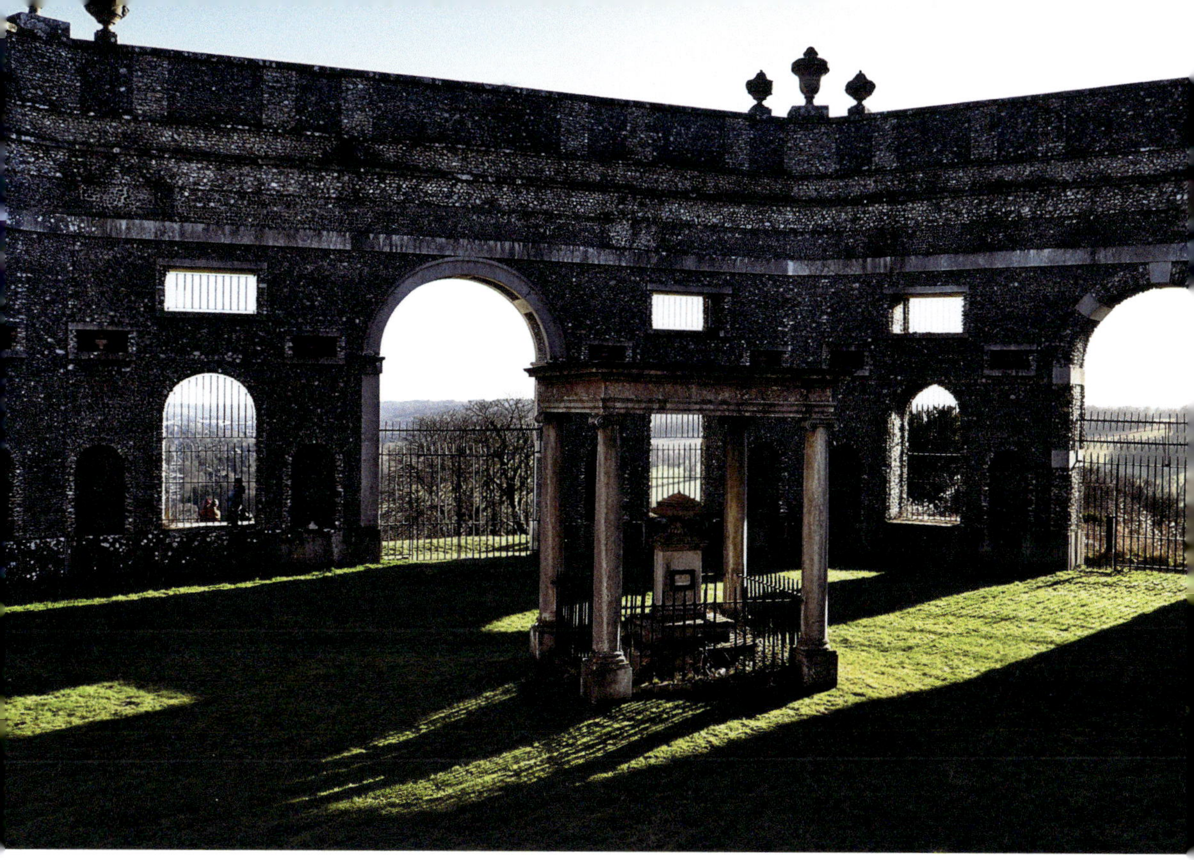

The mausoleum contains many memorials to the Dashwood family.

It is a monumental hexagonal building, open to the sky with massive walls faced with flint inside and out. On its south-eastern side it cuts across part of the surrounding ditch of the hill fort (see West Wycombe Hill Fort). Each side has a vast arch flanked with Tuscan columns along with smaller arches and rectangular openings. Within there are numerous arches and rectangular niches designed to hold memorial slabs and urns. In the centre there is a grand cenotaph consisting of four columns supporting a roof and covering an urn on a pedestal. It commemorates Sir Francis Dashwood's wife, Sarah, Baroness le Despencer, who died in 1769.

Against the north side of the structure there stands a memorial to two Dashwood women: Mary King and Lady Mary Fane. Both were wives of the first Sir Francis who bought West Wycombe Park in 1689. The monument originally stood in the church.

One of the mausoleum's curious memorials is an urn that once contained the heart of the poet Paul Whitehead. He was a close friend of Sir Francis and steward of the Hell Fire Club. He died in 1774 having requested that his heart be placed in an urn within the mausoleum. Unfortunately in 1827 it was stolen by an Australian tourist.

West Wycombe Mausoleum is truly a remarkable building. Yet, strictly speaking, it is not actually a mausoleum. The word mausoleum derives from the last resting place of King Mausolus, King of Anatolia (modern-day Turkey) from 377 to 353 BC and in fact denotes a tomb.

## 30. Church Loft

Church Loft is the oldest standing building in West Wycombe village, possibly dating from around 1465. It is timber framed with a red-brick façade and an overhanging first floor. It also contains a bell turret, and in 1688 a rather fine clock was added overlooking the street. In the eigheenth century it was known as Church House and accommodated pilgrims travelling between London and Oxford.

Throughout its history it has been used as a court, village jail, shop and as a site for the village stocks. On the left-hand side of the building is an arch that leads into Church Lane, which once contained the village lock-up and whipping post. Beautiful and ancient the building is, yet it must have sent the odd shiver down the spine of any villagers who stepped out of line. Today the building is used by the people of the West Wycombe for more friendly village events.

The enjoyment of any building is, for me, not only in its architecture, but its history, or to be more precise the history it has lived through. As we stand in West Wycombe and admire Church Loft, walk its rooms, touch its wood and brick, and take in its ancient atmosphere. It is good to remind ourselves that when it

Church Loft, the oldest building in West Wycombe.

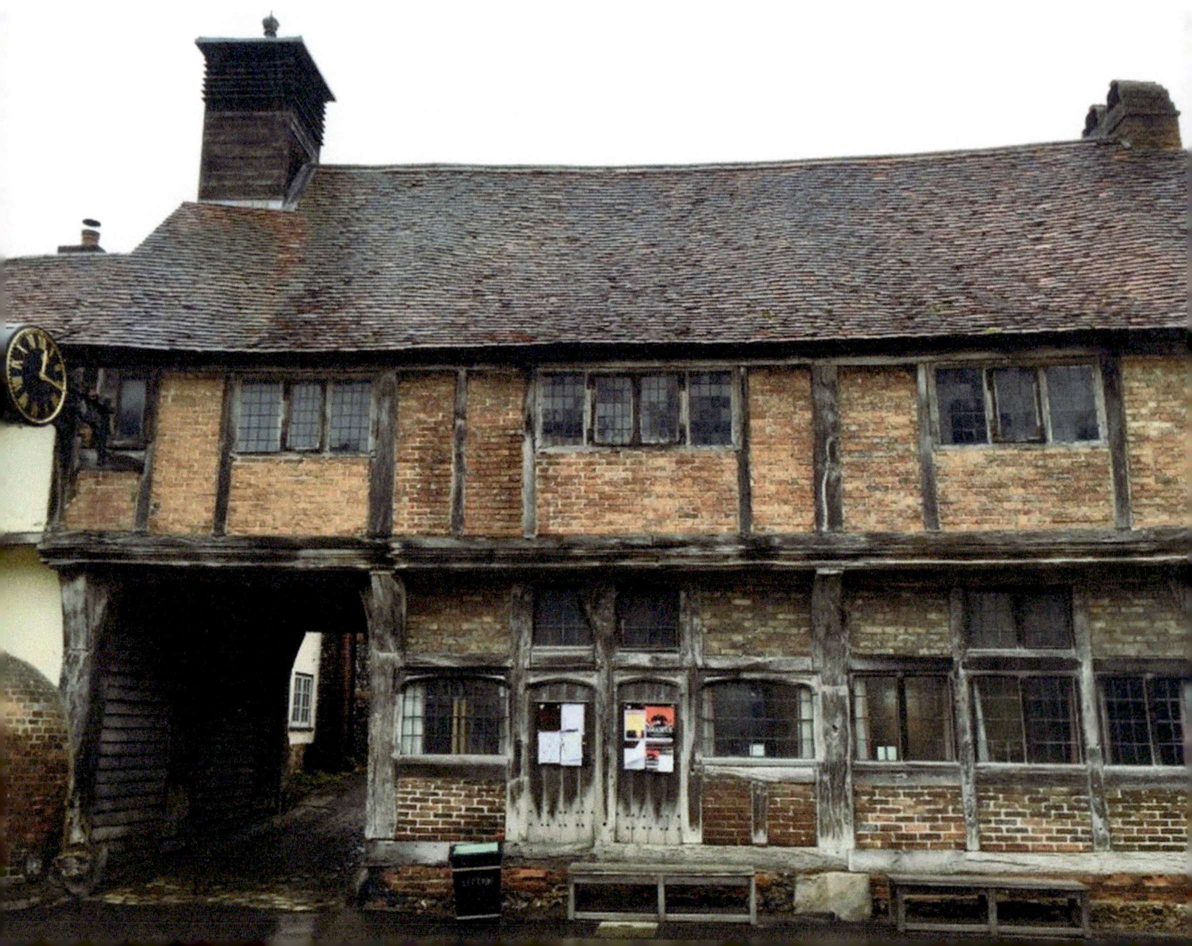

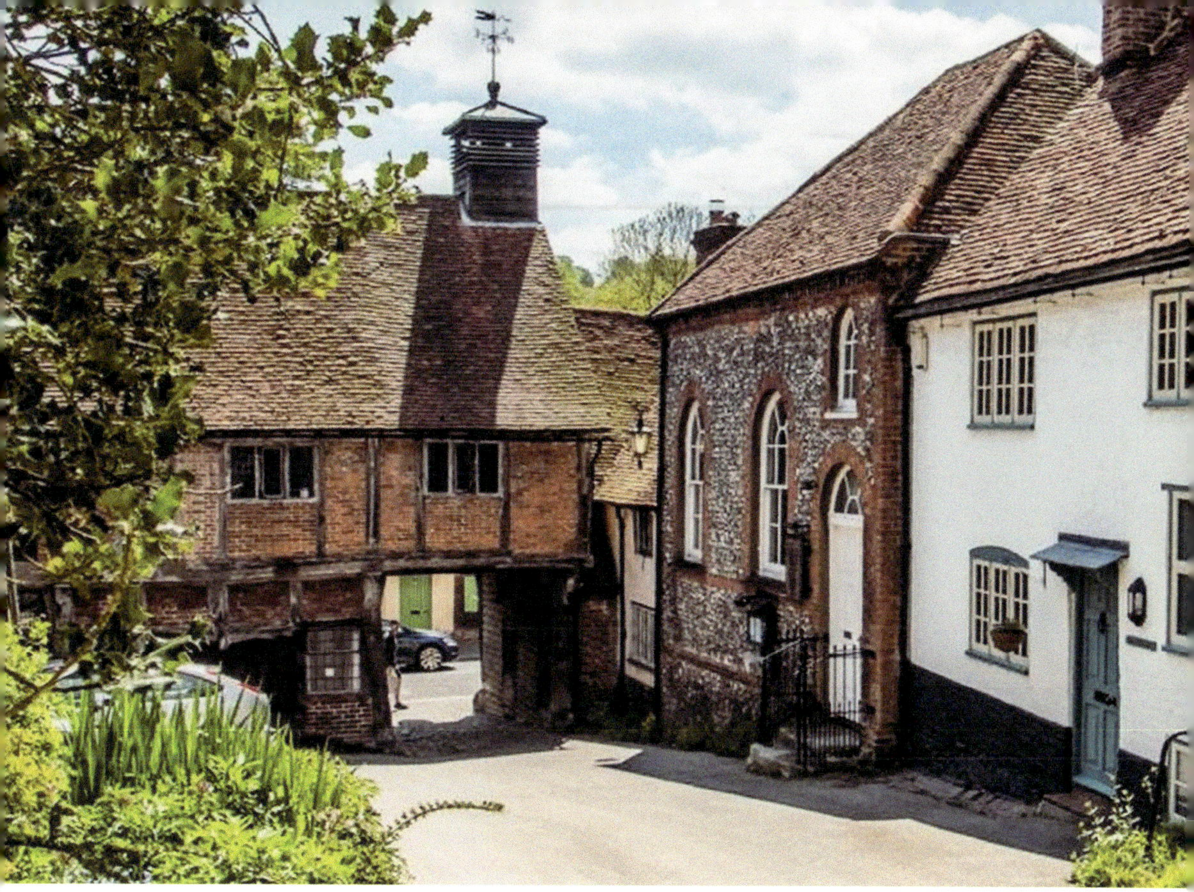

The idyllic rear lane of Church Loft.

was built the Wars of the Roses were raging in England. It was standing during the reigns of Henry VIII and Elizabeth I. By the time of the Gunpowder Plot it was already 130 years old. During the English Civil War its windows would have looked down on Roundheads or Cavaliers marching along the street. Perhaps the next time you pass through West Wycombe you won't look upon Church Loft as just another old building.

## 31. West Wycombe Gardens

The great appeal of many of England's stately mansions and houses is not only the architecture of the buildings themselves, their histories and the treasures they contain, but also the beautiful gardens in which they stand. I use the word garden loosely here, for although they are technically 'gardens' a more apt description would be 'imagined, romantic landscapes'. Perhaps the most well known in England are Stourhead in Wiltshire, and Stowe in North Buckinghamshire.

Although modest in comparative size, the gardens at West Wycombe are of equal importance and beauty. The park was created by Sir Francis Dashwood from

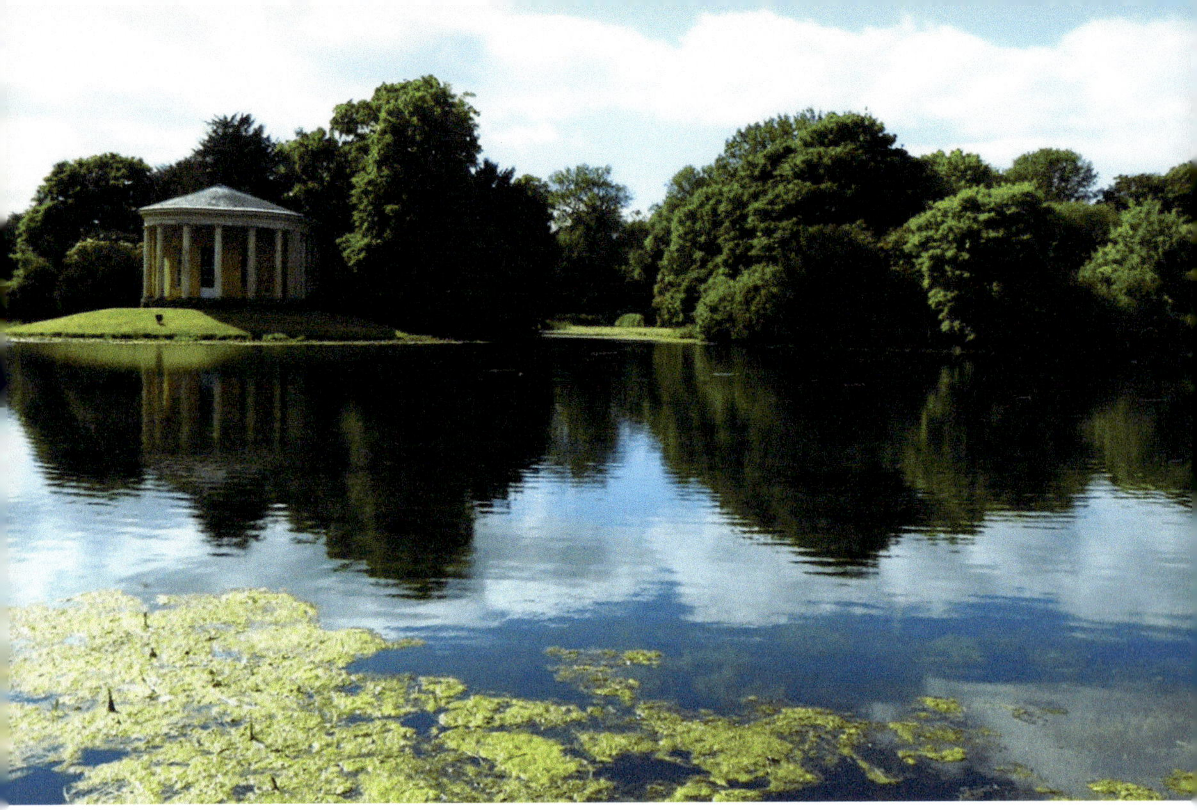

*Above*: The beautiful classical gardens at West Wycombe Park.

*Below*: The gardens are dotted with many follies and temples.

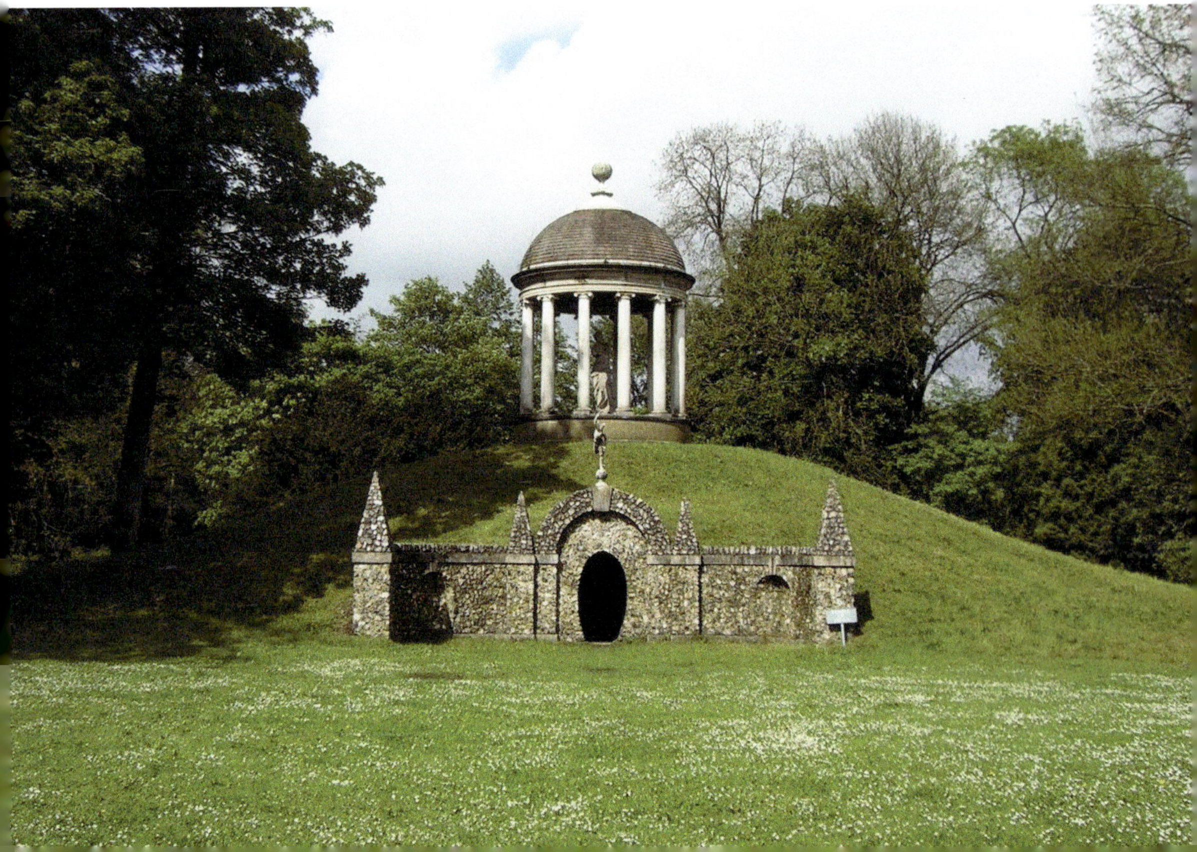

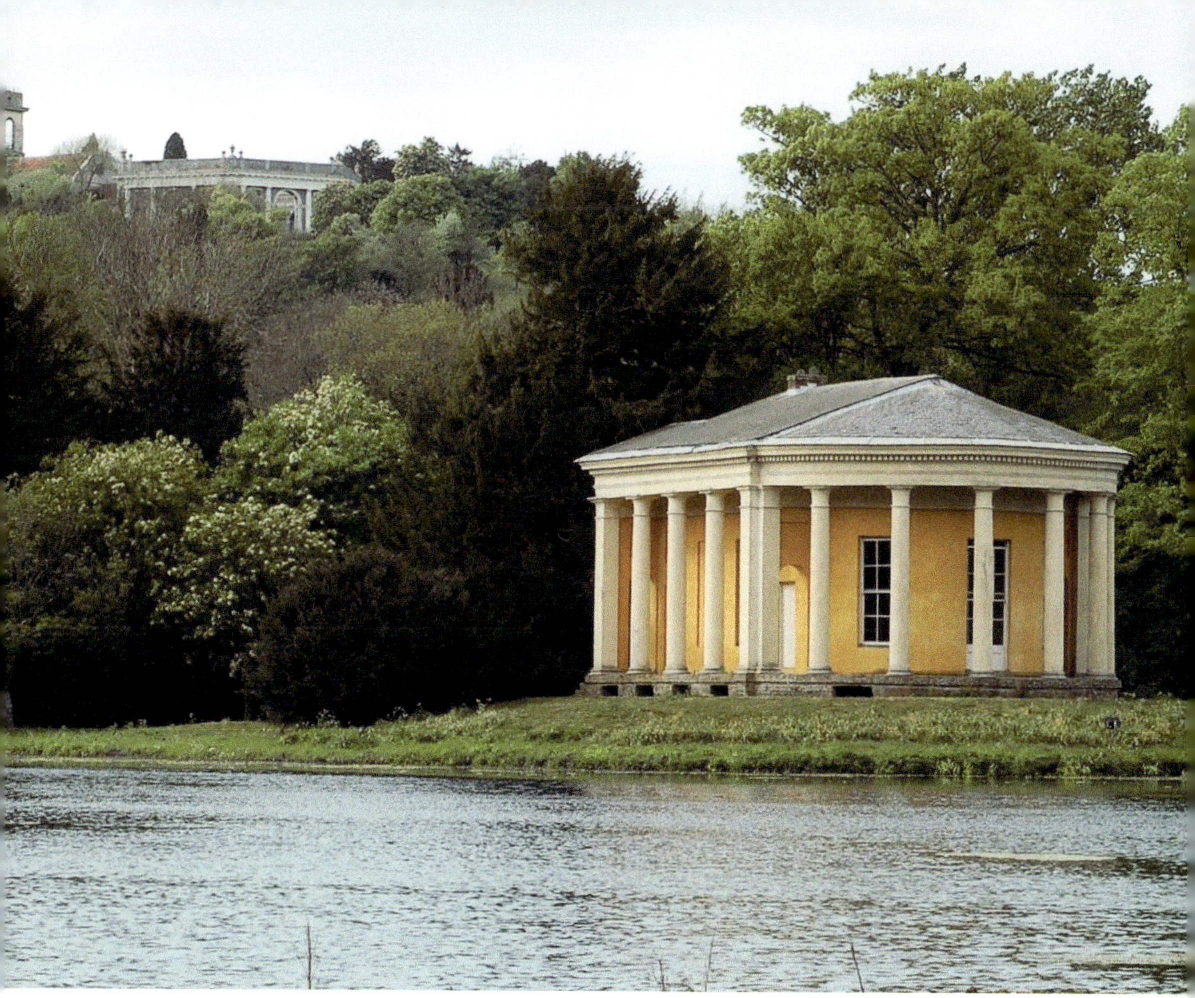

The Temple of Music at West Wycombe Park.

the mid to late eighteenth century, and is unique in its constant use of classical architecture from Greece and Italy. The classical theme runs through the garden, with follies, pavilions, grottoes, winding paths and classical statues at every turn. They include the Temple of Music on an island in the lake, and the Temple of Apollo, once used as a cockfighting venue.

The gardens stretch over 5,000 acres and are arranged in a series of walks that take the visitor through a range of locations each separate from the last, yet harmonious in their pleasant vistas and set pieces. The names of the follies reflect Dashwood's interest in classical mythology, shown in titles such as 'Temple of the Four Winds', 'Temple of Daphne' and the 'Temple of St Crispin'.

The gardens are open to the public, and yet walking through this timeless, peaceful eighteenth-century landscape, it is hard to imagine that the hustle and bustle of twenty-first-century High Wycombe is just a lengthy stone's throw away. If you require an escape from the madness of the modern world, head for Sir Francis Dashwood's glorious backyard.

## 32. West Wycombe Park

The origins of West Wycombe Park go back to the late seventeenth century when the first Francis Dashwood built a house on the site in 1698. In 1724, he died, and his only son, also Francis, inherited the estate and the Baronetcy of West Wycombe. The second baronet set about demolishing the original house and building a grand Italianate mansion.

Dashwood's design for the house was much influenced by his travels in Europe. During the eighteenth century it was fashionable for landed gentry and gentlemen to go on the grand tour. They returned to England with sumptuous ideas for classical architecture. Dashwood's mansion was built and added to between 1740 and 1800 and encapsulates the entire progression of British eighteenth-century architecture from Palladian to neoclassical. It is set within a landscape park containing many follies and temples, a fashionable practise at the time in landscaped English gardens (see West Wycombe Gardens).

West Wycombe House, compared with other great stately mansions of England, is quite modest in size, yet it is architecturally important for it was built at a time when the obligatory grand tour saw young men of means return with acquisitions of art and a suitable place to accommodate and display their collections. The interior contains a series of rooms decorated with classical scenes from Greek and Roman mythology, while the entrance hall reassembles a Roman atrium (a large open-air space or skylight) with marbled columns and a painted ceiling showing the ruins of Palmyra in Syria.

The finest chamber is the Music Room. Despite the name, the room has always been used for lavish balls. Its ceiling is decorated with a superb painting by Giuseppe Borgnis, who also painted the Blue Drawing Room and Yellow Saloon. Perhaps the height of West Wycombe's social standing was when the Tapestry Room was used as a bedroom by George III on a state visit.

When Sir Francis died in 1781 it seemed like the heady days of West Wycombe Park were over. The estate passed to his half-brother, Sir John Dashwood King. He spent little time at the house and on his death in 1793 it was inherited by his son, Sir John Dashwood, who cared little for the mansion. In 1800 he sold off most of the furniture and would have sold the house if not prevented by his son, to whom the estate was entailed (a deed that restricts the sale of an inherited property). Sir John died in 1849, bankrupt and estranged form his wife.

In 1922 another Sir John Dashwood, the 10th Baronet, tried to sell the house, but the only offer of £10,000 was rejected. Because of debts he sold off most of the remaining furniture. He ultimately ended up living in a house he disliked, allowing parts to be abandoned and decay.

During the Second World War the house was used as a depositary for the Wallace Collection, no doubt to save it from German bombs. Soldiers occupied one of the wings, while the Dashwoods were forced to use only the upper floors. To pay the bills lodgers were taken in.

After the war the house and grounds were given to the National Trust on condition that the Dashwoods and their descendants could continue to live there. Happily, today the fortunes and future of West Wycombe Park are secure and are open to the public.

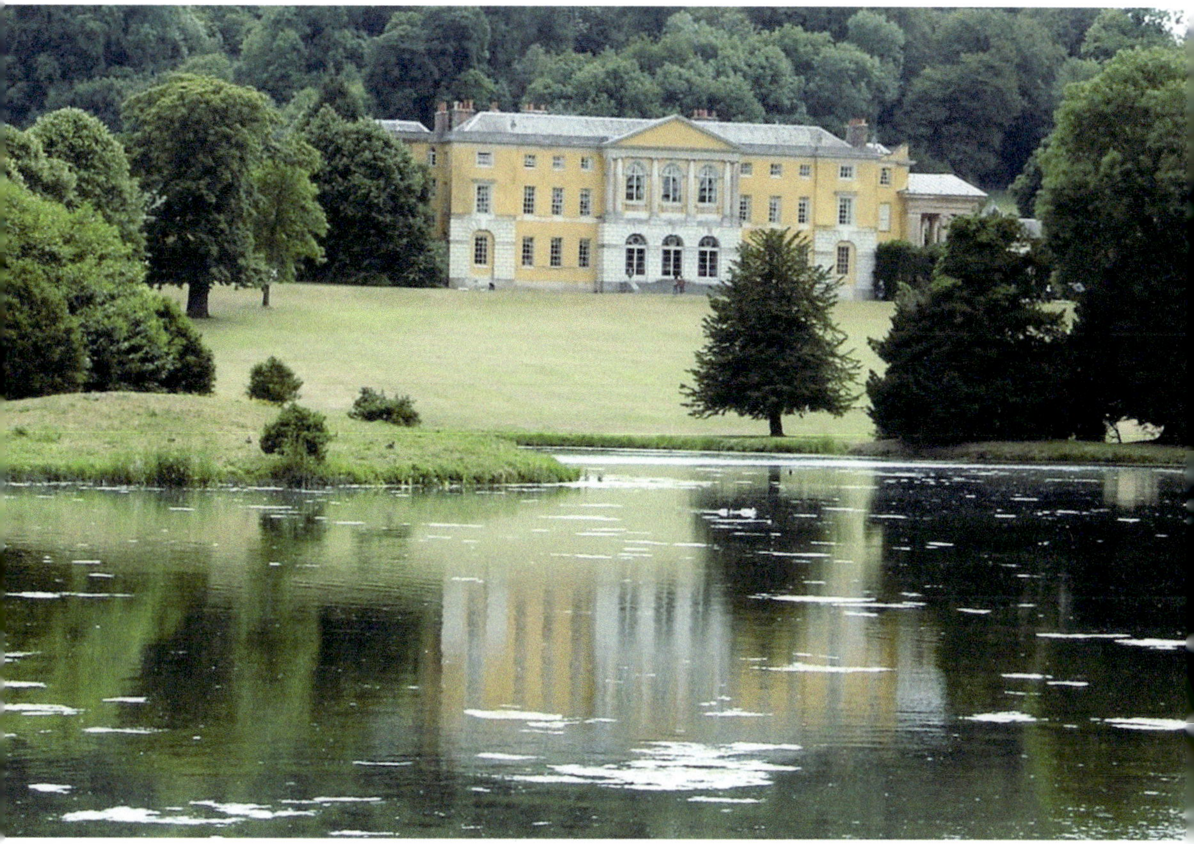

*Above*: The grand front of West Wycombe Park, home to the Dashwood family.

*Right*: The entrance hall at West Wycombe.

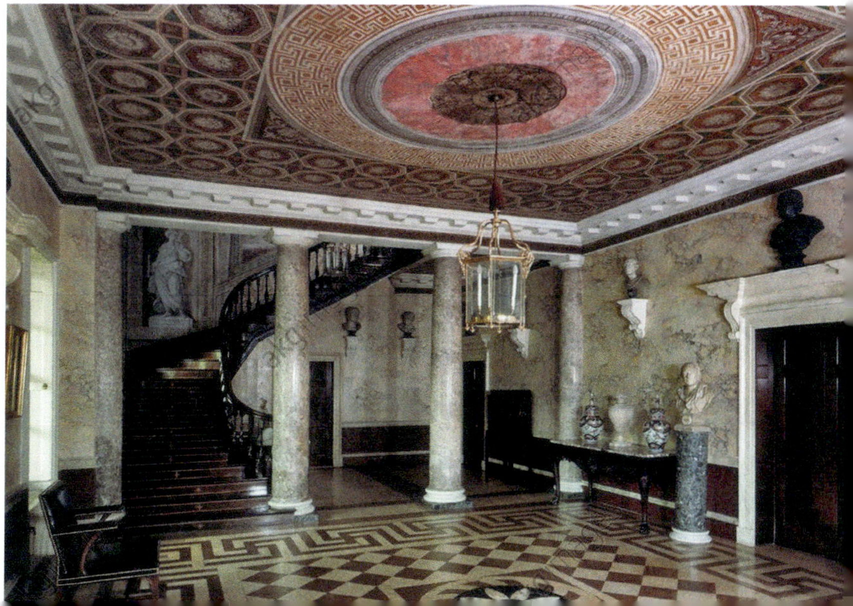

## 33. Hell Fire Caves

Sir Francis Dashwood was a man of many contrasts. On one side he was a politician and Member of Parliament who, although a dreadful chancellor, was a competent postmaster general. Together with his friend, American Benjamin Franklin, he produced a revised Book of Common Prayer. The book was ignored in England, but subsequently used in America. He was also a great supporter of the working men and farm hands of the area. Following three years of successive harvest failures between 1748 and 1750, Dashwood provided work for the

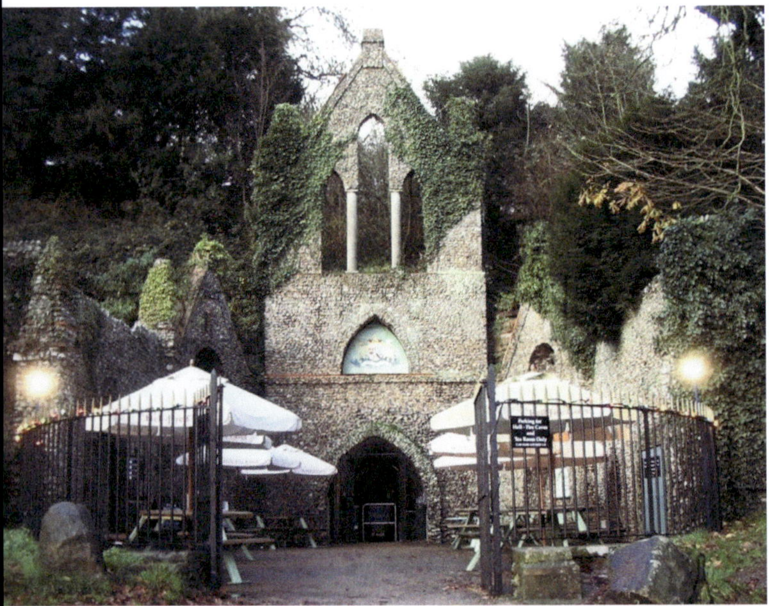

*Left*: The Gothic entrance to West Wycombe Caves.

*Below*: Mannequins of Sir Francis Dashwood and Benjamin Franklin explore the caves.

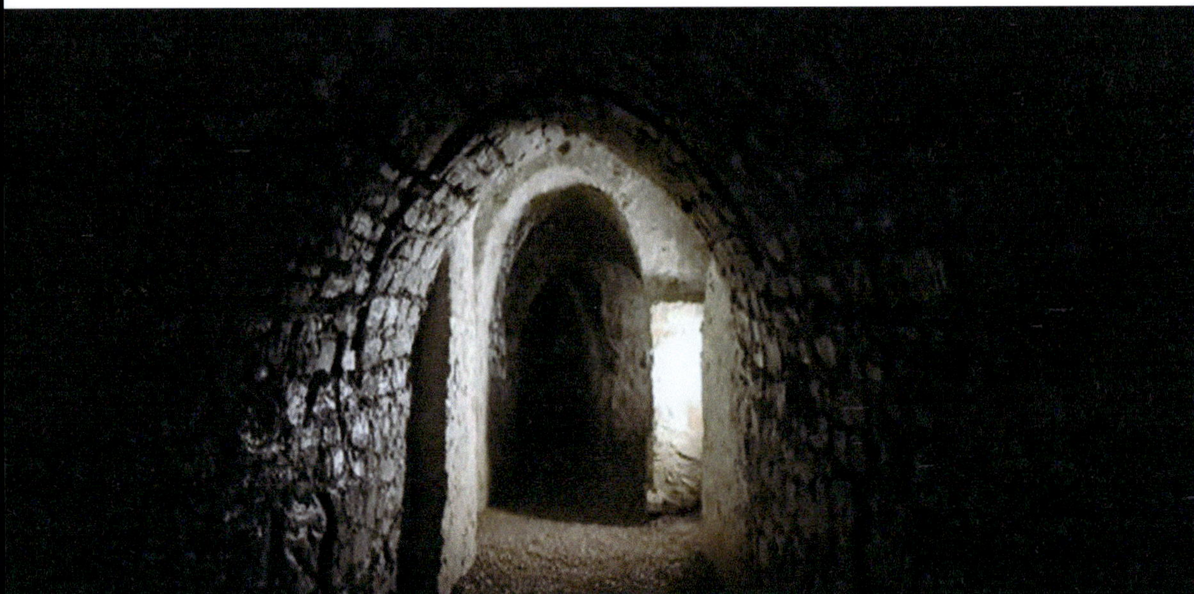

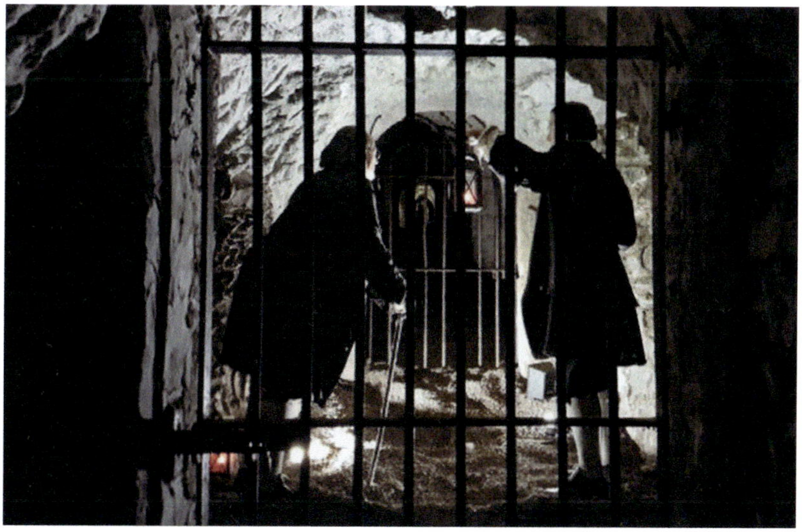

The eerie interior of the Hell Fire Caves.

unemployed constructing and improving a road between West Wycombe and High Wycombe. Yet hidden behind this smiling philanthropy was another side to the baronet: the pleasure-seeking rake who, with his friends, indulged in all manner of scandalous behaviour.

The Monks of Medmenham, later to be known as the Hell Fire Club, first gathered at the ruined medieval abbey of Medmenham on the banks of the River Thames some 8 miles south of West Wycombe in 1753. However, the club would in time switch the venue for their drunken get-togethers to the caves below West Wycombe Hill.

West Wycombe Caves had, for many centuries, been used as a chalk quarry. It is believed that as far back as prehistoric times a cave snaked its way under the hill. With the breakup of the first Hell Fire Club at Medmenham and local harvest failures, Dashwood took the opportunity to use unemployed Wycombe men to excavate the caves for the material for a new road, yet also to indulge his fancy for a new venue for the Hell Fire members.

The entrance to the caves is fronted by a mock ruined church façade, which was originally built to be viewed from the grounds of West Wycombe House. The tunnels and passageways descend their way under the hill for a distance of 400 metres, and are romantically described as the Hall of Statues, the treasure chamber and Whitehead's Cave. The labyrinth carries on to an underground pool, which Dashwood named the River Styx (in Greek mythology the River Styx separated the mortal world from the realm of the dead. One could only cross it by paying Charon, the ferryman. Once across the pool the members of the club entered the Inner Temple, a chamber used by senior Hell Fire associates for drinking and frolics with their lady guests.

After Dashwood's death in 1781, aged seventy-three, the caves fell out of use. Yet during the Blitz on Britain during the Second World War, they were used as an air-raid shelter. It wasn't until 1951 that they were reopened to the public as a tourist attraction, and it is in this capacity that they remain today.

## 34. St Lawrence's Church, West Wycombe

There are a number of buildings in West Wycombe that not only show the eighteenth-century disdain for the established church of the day, but also the eccentricities and peculiarities of the landed gentry.

The Church of St Lawrence was built between the thirteenth and fourteenth centuries, on the summit of Church Hill. However, given the centuries old religious significance of West Wycombe Hill (see West Wycombe Hill Fort) it is probable that an earlier Saxon place of worship stood on the site. It is thought it originally served the village of Haveringdon, which no longer exists.

The present church is really a building with two histories. The early medieval work is still visible in the rough masonry of the west tower, the thirteenth-century chancel and the remaining feint tracery of its Gothic east window. The interior, however, is a different matter altogether. It is an extraordinary, opulent and ultimately ironic reordering of a church interior.

When lord of the manor,Sir Francis Dashwood returned to England from his grand tour of Europe in 1761 he set about remodelling the interior of St Lawrence's Church with designs based on the classical architecture of Rome and Greece.

Many church interiors in England had, from the late sixteenth century, undergone radical changes to their layout following the introduction of the Book of Common Prayer during the reign of Edward VI (1547–53). Orders were given that all Catholic and popish superstitious imagery and practices were to be removed from the church. Alters, stained glass, statues, carvings and wall paintings depicting the saints were destroyed to be replaced with the plain, sober, box pew interior of English Protestantism.

St Lawrence's Church must have resembled this when Dashwood took off for his grand tour. Yet Sir Francis, perhaps with his tongue in his cheek, seems to have flown in the face of this new liturgical layout and took his church back beyond medieval superstition.

He rebuilt the church in the popular classical manner of the day, heightening the tower and topping it with a golden globe large enough for his cronies to sit and get drunk in. He removed the arcades and replaced them with rich Corinthian columns painted in an imitation exotic marble. The walls are decorated with a palm frieze in the rococo style with garlands, flowers and doves. The lavish decorated ceiling is based on drawings of the pagan temple of the sun at Palmyra in Syria, while the chancel ceiling is adorned by a painting of the last supper. It seemed like a bizarre combination of Christianity and paganism. It was, to one visitor, 'A very superb Egyptian hall'.

For us today it must seem extraordinary how anyone could be allowed to redesign a church in such a fashion. Or was it Dashwood, in his own whimsical, aesthetic manner, sticking two fingers up to the Church of England?

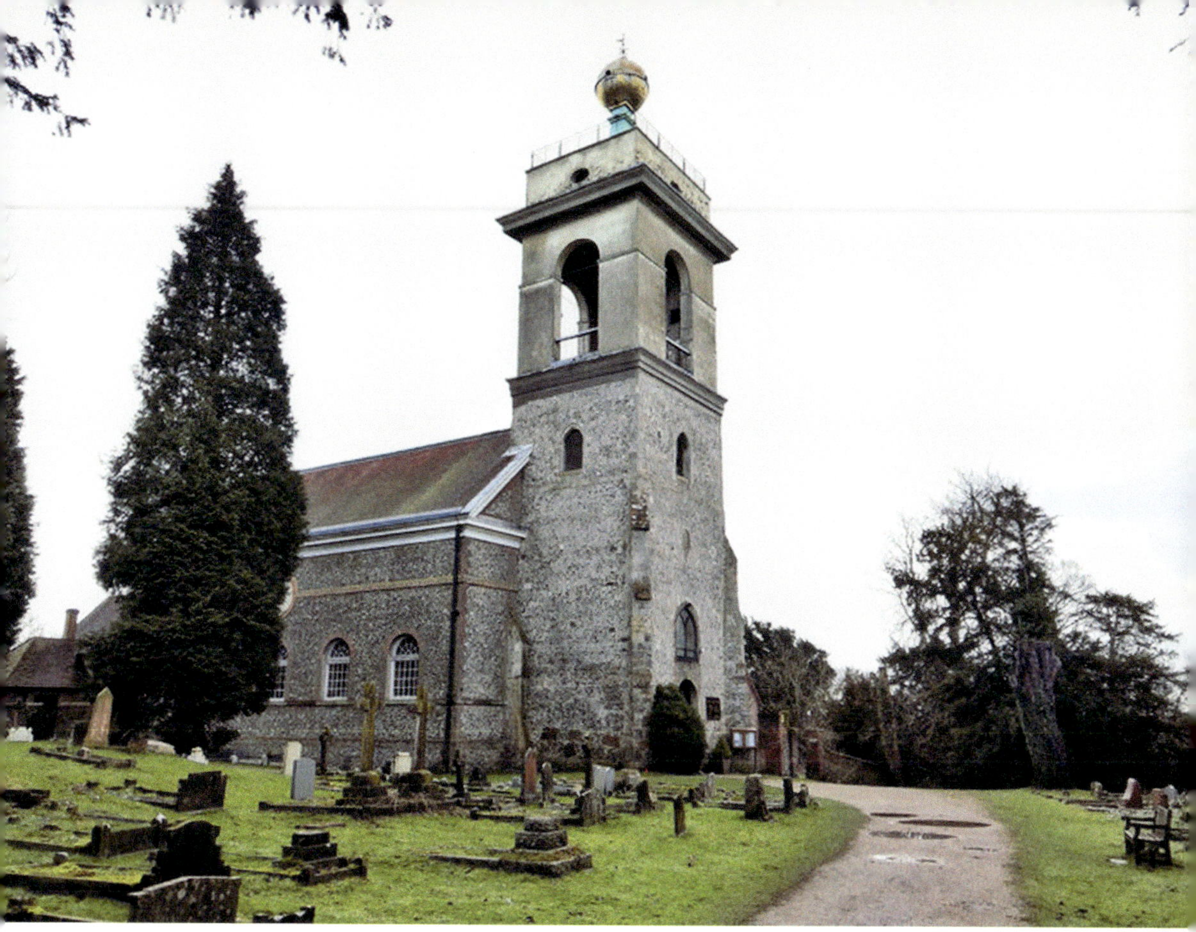

*Above*: The medieval St Lawrence's Church with its golden ball. It was completely altered by Dashwood in the eighteenth century.

*Right*: The magnificent interior of St Lawrence's.

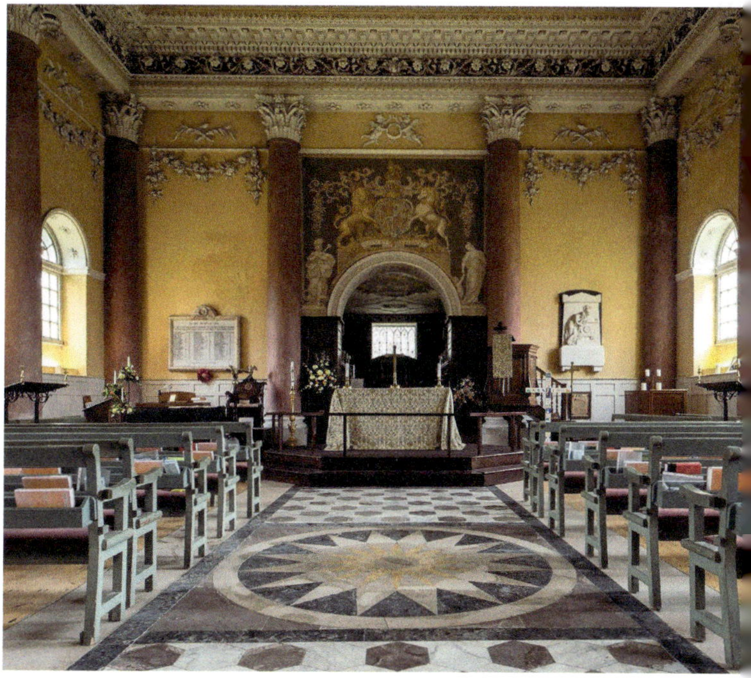

## 35. Holy Trinity Church, Penn

Strictly speaking, Holy Trinity Church is not in High Wycombe. The village it provides with spiritual guidance is Penn, which lies some 3 miles from the centre of the town. However, although it retains its rural setting, Penn, at least on its western fringes, has seen the fingers of Wycombe's urban expansion creep ever closer, and to some degree has become part suburban.

Nonetheless, the importance of Holy Trinity Church, not only to High Wycombe but also to Buckinghamshire, and indeed the wider world, is too significant to omit from this book.

Like many of England's ancient churches, Holy Trinity is a product of centuries of change and development. It dates from the twelfth century, although it is entirely possible that a Saxon place of worship had previously stood on the site. The building is composed of a nave, south aisle, chancel and a solid, short west tower. The chancel was remodelled in 1733, yet many of its eighteenth-century furnishings would have been replaced during the Victorian area. However, the pulpit dates from the remodelling, and originally came for the Curzon Street chapel in London. The Curzon family were responsible for restoring the church.

The interior of All Saints Church.

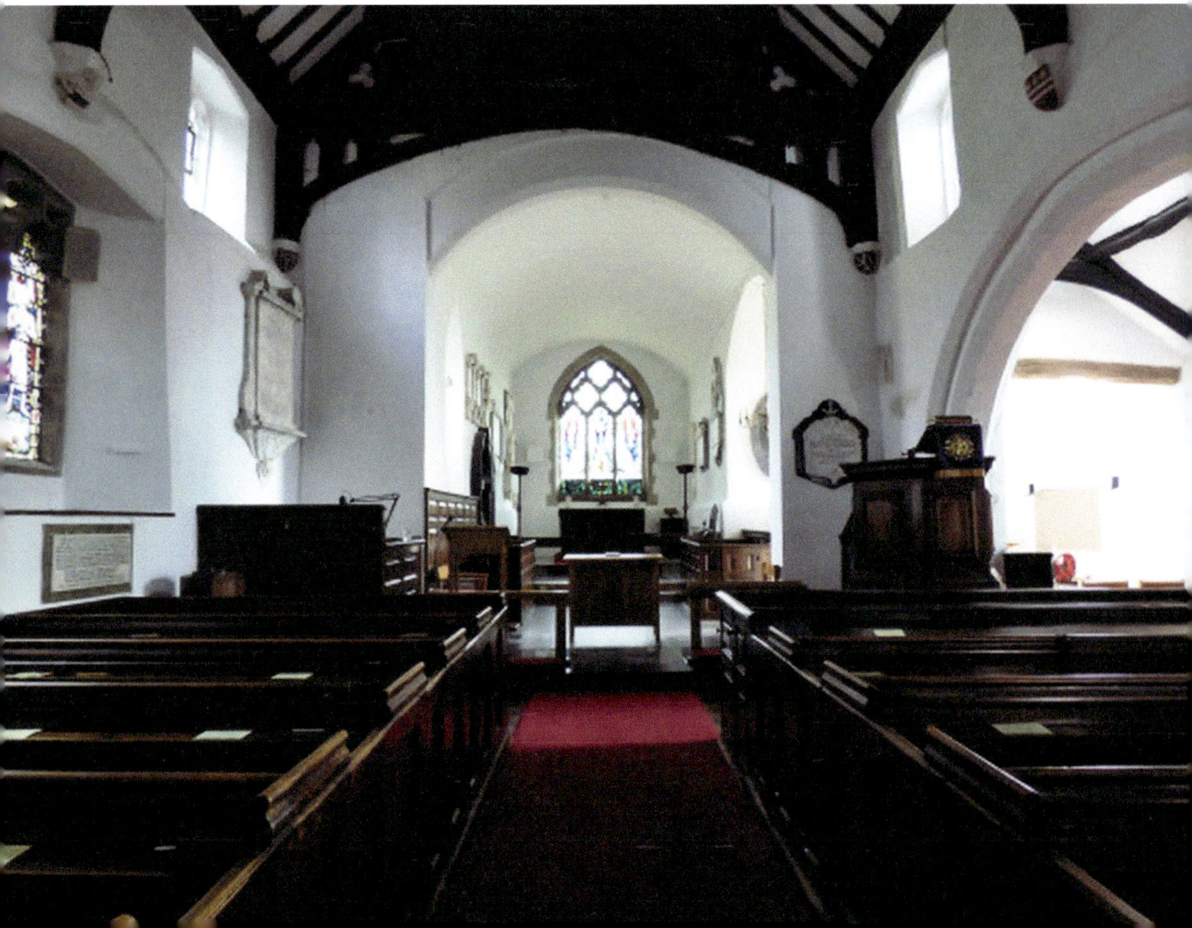

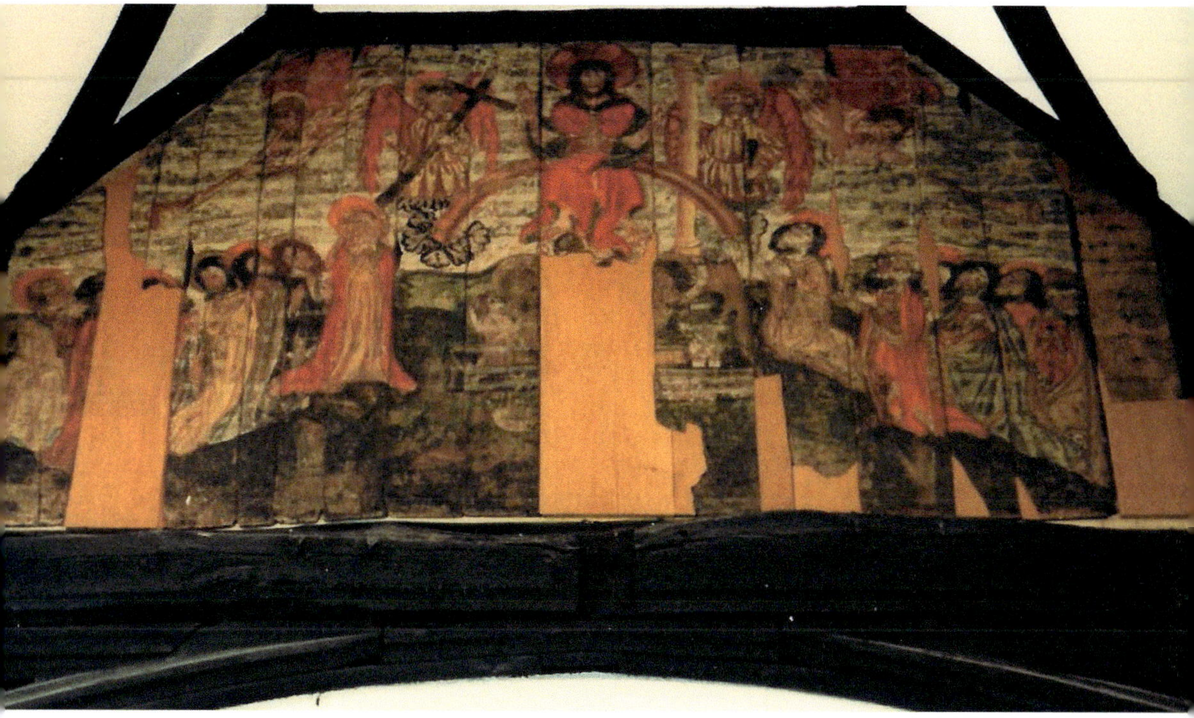

The fifteenth-century doom painting above the chancel arch.

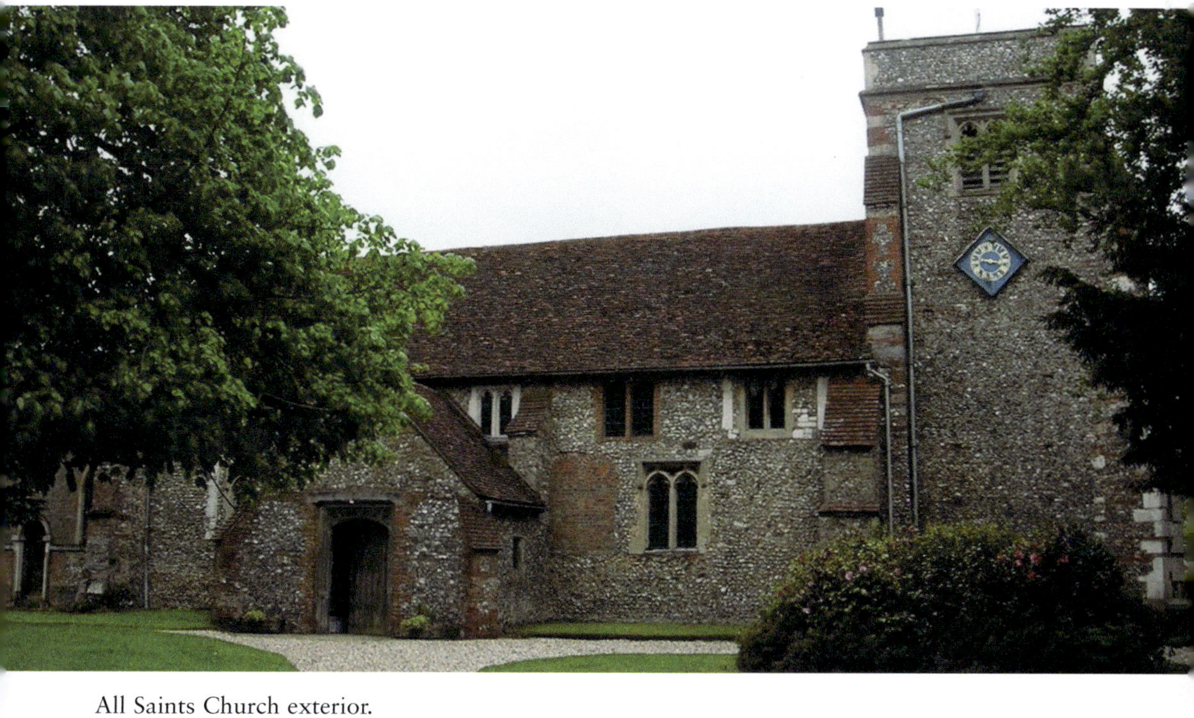

All Saints Church exterior.

The interior contains a rare fifteenth-century doom painting on oak panels above the chancel arch. Doom paintings depicted Judgement Day when Christ would come and judge those who were worthy of a place in Heaven, and also those sinners who were destined to fiery Hell. It is thought to be one of only five such doom paintings on boards to survive in England.

Perhaps the most interesting aspect of the church are the families connected to the village and those who lie in Holy Trinity churchyard. Six grandsons of Sir William Penn, founder of Pennsylvania in America, lie within the vaults, and their memorials are dotted around the church. Sir William Penn established the city of Philadelphia, recognised as the first capital of the United States. Penn claimed the village and Buckinghamshire as his ancestral home.

Within the churchyard are two graves with, perhaps, a less than noble but nonetheless intriguing history. Here one can find the last resting place of David Blakeley. He was murdered outside a London pub in 1953 by Ruth Ellis. She was found guilty and became the last woman in Britain to be hanged. Nearby are the graves of the Maclean family. Their son, Donald, was a British diplomat who was one of the Cambridge Five spy ring, which conveyed secrets to the Soviet Union shortly after the Second World War. He was discovered but defected to Russia in 1951. In 1983 he died and requested that his ashes be returned to England and scattered on his parents' grave in Penn churchyard.

## 36. Bradenham Manor

Bradenham lies some 2 miles north of the outskirts of Wycombe on the road to Princes Risborough. It is a pleasant location with a handful of cottages, church and rather large village green. Its chief attraction is the manor house. The current house was built by Sir Edmund Plie, who was a Member of Parliament and sat in the House of Commons from 1661 to 1673. It dates to around the late seventeenth century. Yet there has been a building on this site since the thirteenth century that belonged to the Earls of Warwick.

In 1556 Queen Elizabeth I was entertained at Bradenham by Lord Windsor, one of the hereditary wardens of Windsor Castle. The house remained the property of the Windsor family until 1642, when it was acquired by Sir Edmund Pile. It was once again sold in 1787 to a John Hicks. When Hicks died in 1825 the ownership of the house was contested and remained in chancery (dispute).

Although the manor was in ownership limbo, it was still leased to a number of tenants, one of whom was Isaac Disraeli, the father of eminent Victorian politician Benjamin Disraeli. As a young man Benjamin spent much time at Bradenham and developed a lifelong love of Buckinghamshire and the Chilterns. When his father died in 1848, Disraeli had to leave Bradenham, yet he would not have to travel very far to find his own stately residence. The same year he acquired the house which would become his home until his death: Hughenden Manor (see Hughenden).

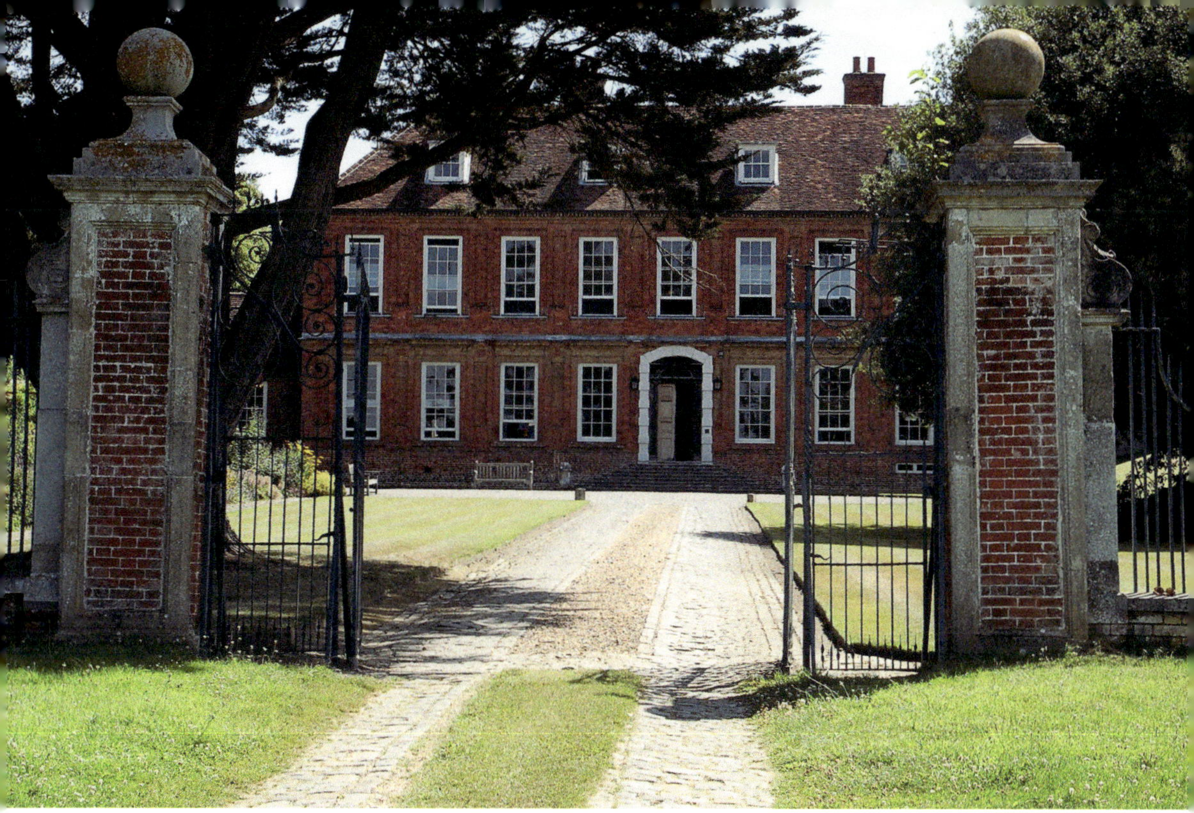

*Above*: The entrance to the stately Bradenham Manor.

*Below*: Bradenham Manor and church.

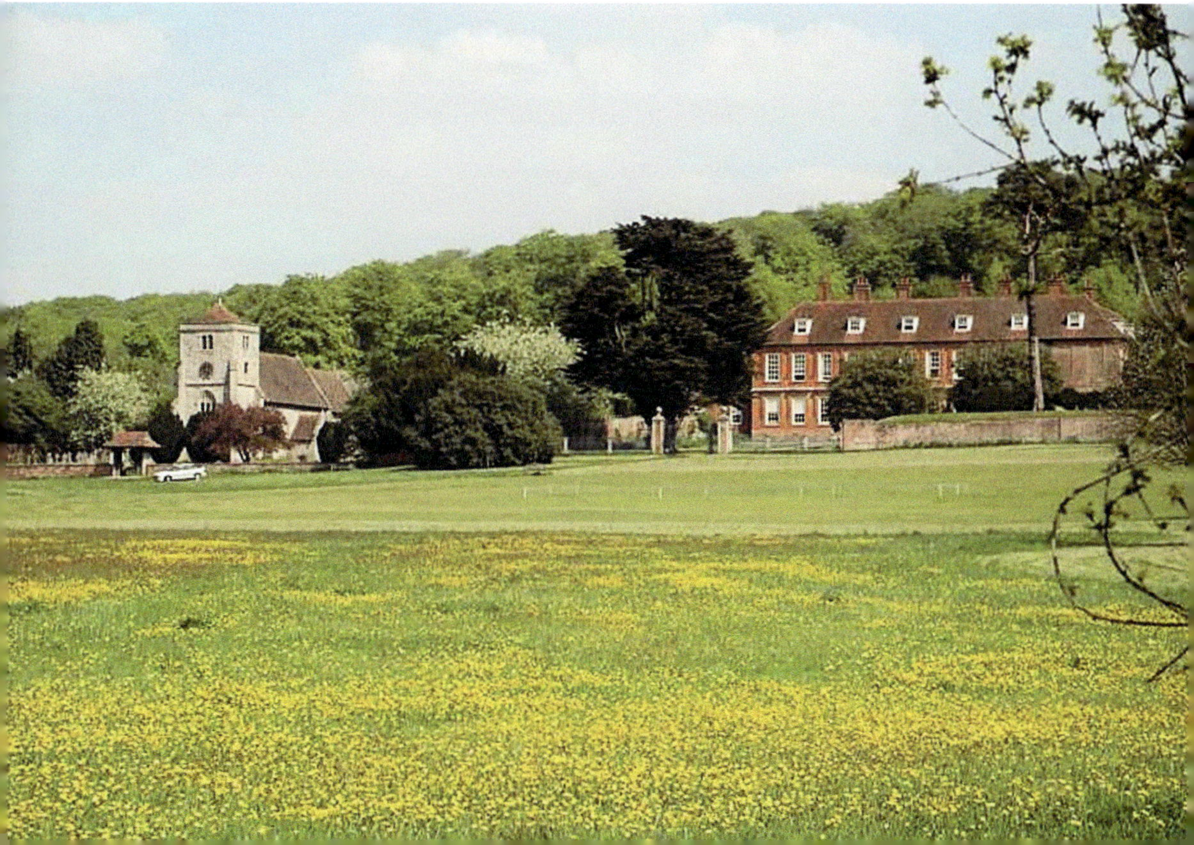

## 37. RAF High Wycombe

Despite its name, RAF High Wycombe lies some 3 miles from the town in the village of Walters Ash. It was designed in the late 1930s to house Bomber Command. The station's location was originally suggested by Wing Commander Alan Oakeshott. Prior to the outbreak of the Second World War the Air Ministry sought a new, secure site for Bomber Command away from London and the threat of German bombs. The wooded area around Walters Ash, Naphill and Lacey Green was sufficiently located inland and also within a densely wooded area, which provided natural camouflage from the air.

To further disguise the station from German reconnaissance the officers' mess was built to resemble a manor house, and the fire station designed to look like a church. Tunnels connected each block on the site all linked to an operations block that was 55 feet below ground.

Although it was not an official flying station, between 1844 and late 1945 a small airfield was used in the nearby village of Lacey Green. During the war the

RAF High Wycombe. Today it is guarded by a Spitfire and a Hurricane.

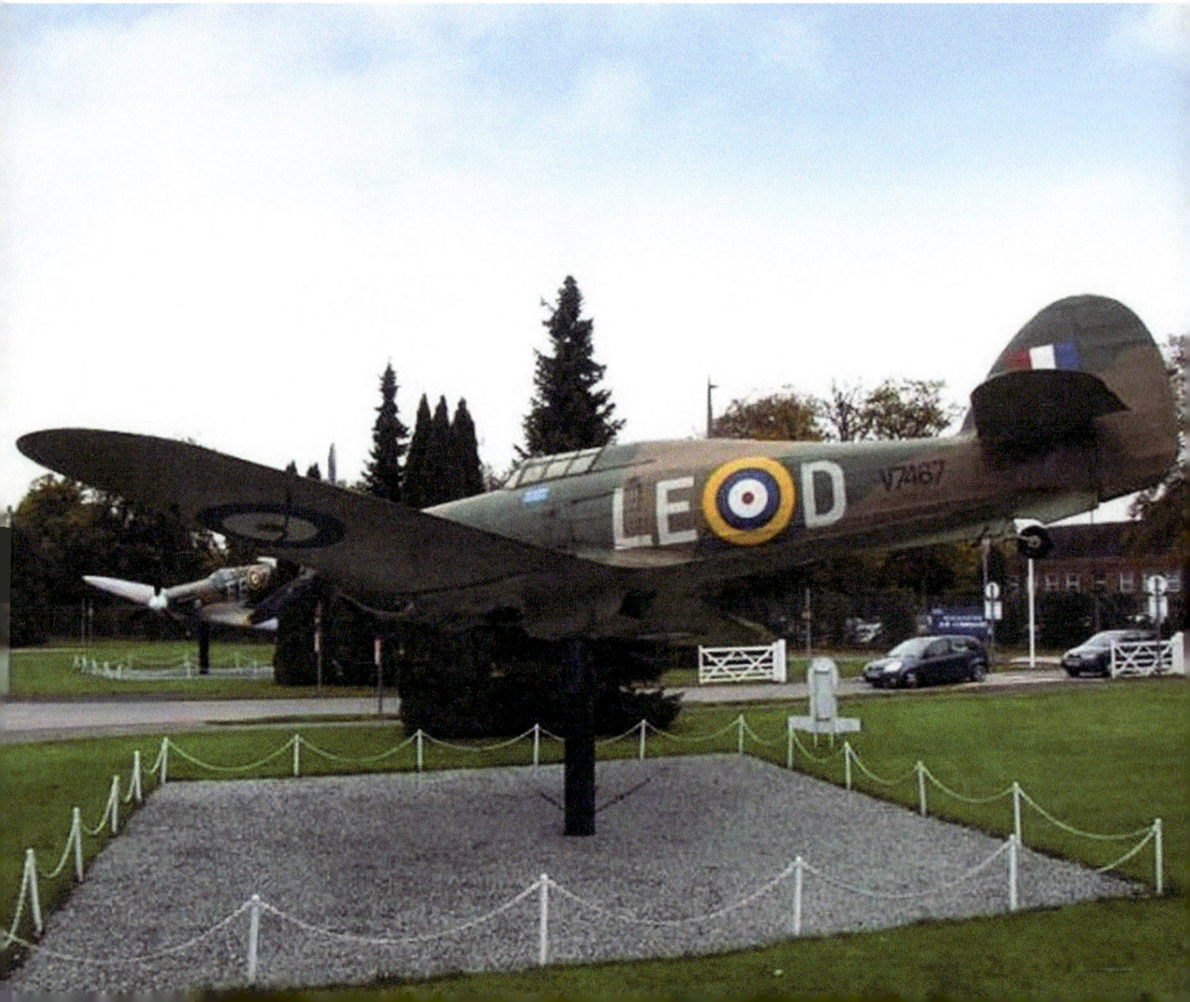

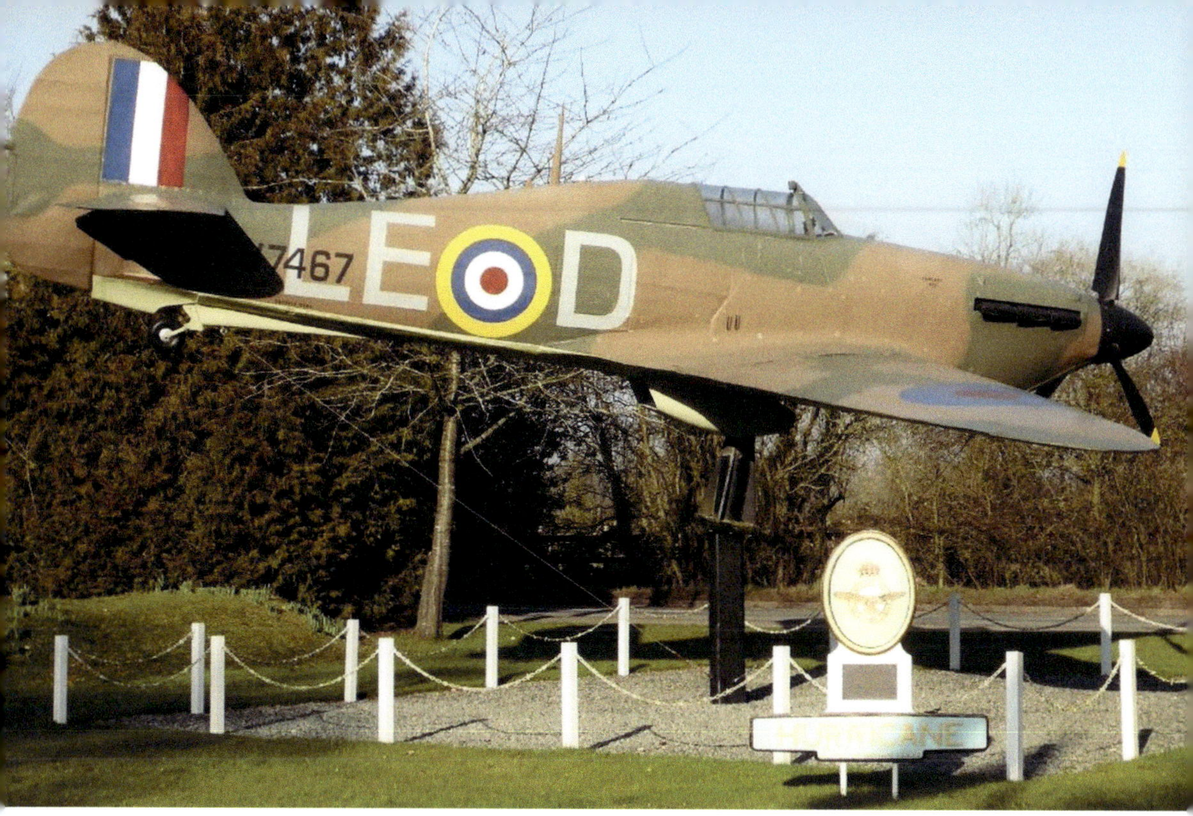


A Spitfire at RAF High Wycombe.

station was not only home to Bomber Command, but also the 325th Photographic Wing, United States Air Forces.

After the end of the Second World War the station became an important part of Britain's defence. During the Cold War it was assumed that the Strike Command Operational Centre nuclear bunker was located at RAF Wycombe. It was here that the four-minute warning for a nuclear attack would have been acted upon. In fact the real command centre was at Goosnargh, near Preston, in the north of England.

In 1958, Strategic Air Command was relocated from RAF South Ruislip to Wycombe. The station was headquarters for all SAC operations until 1965. In 1994 it became the headquarters of NATO, Allied Forces North Western Europe.

## 38. Brands House

Brands House stands tucked away on a back road between Terriers and Widmer End. It is an imposing Grade II listed country mansion dating from the eighteenth and nineteenth centuries. It was once the centre of a 730-acre estate, and although much of its surrounding farmland has been sold off, it remains in an impressive parkland setting.

The name Brand is an ancient one, and is believed to date back to the twelfth century when a landowner of Old English and Scandinavian descent by the name of Brand held land in the area. The earliest part of the house still standing is the west wing, which was built about 1770. The main part of the house was constructed in the early nineteenth century by the Newman family, who owned the property until 1919. John Newman was an eminent gentleman and JP sitting on the bench at the same time as Disraeli.

When the estate was sold in 1919 it comprised a substantial country estate that had been built up by the Newman family. It was purchased by the Vicars family and became known for its shooting parties and point to point horse racing. Sadly the last of the Vicars family vacated Brands in 1978 and the house fell into disrepair. Part of its parkland, along with its outlying buildings, were sold off. The house eventually became offices, but suffered neglect.

Today it is once more a family home. It has been restored and, together with its prominent south facing parkland, has regained some of its former glory.

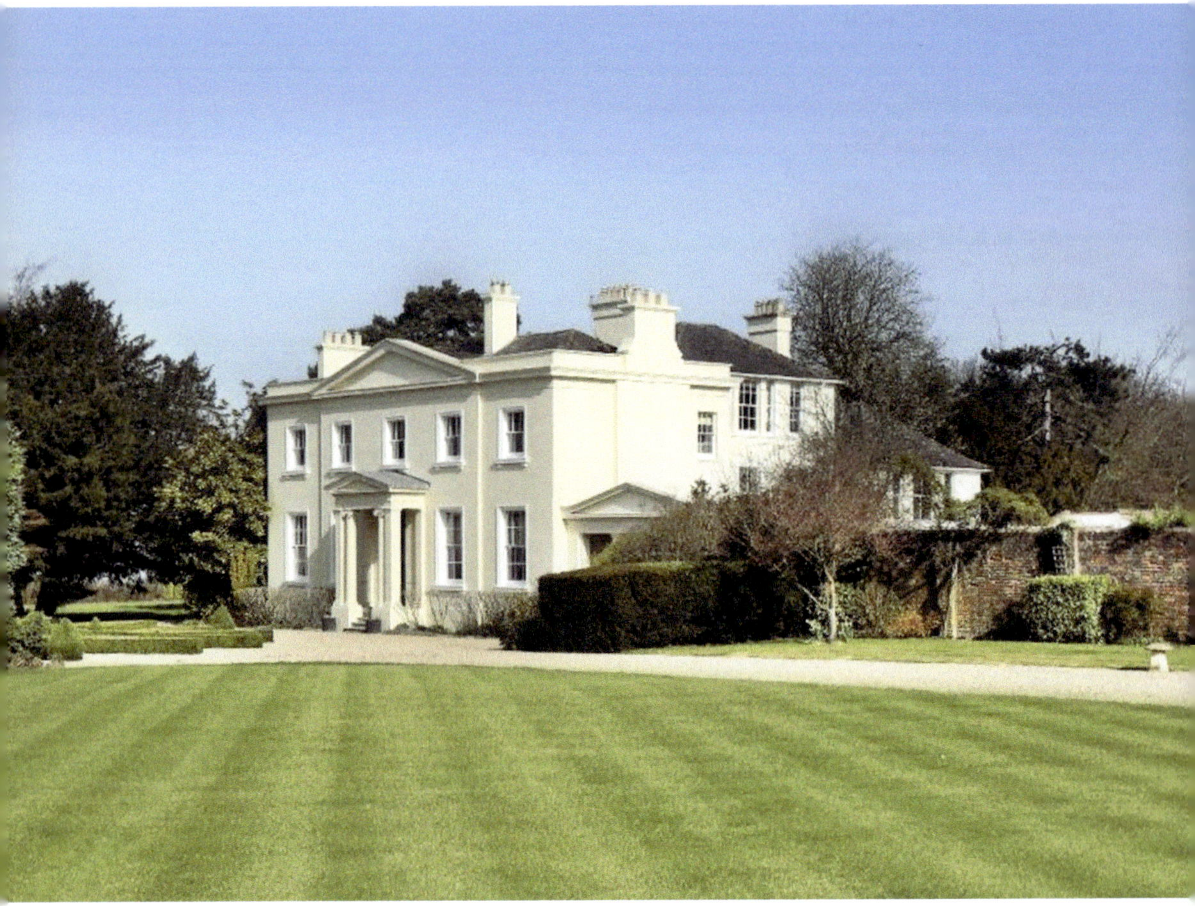

The grand front of Brands House in Widmer End.

## 39. St Margaret's Church, Tylers Green

American Anglophile author Bill Bryson once observed that it is impossible to walk more than a mile in Britain without coming across something interesting and worth giving some time to explore and contemplate. More often than not we pass by these little nuggets of our history completely unaware of their presence. The building nineteen in this book refers to Magdala House on Terriers Green, where one of Britain's greatest pioneers of aviation was born. Likewise, just outside the centre of Wycombe is the village of Tylers Green. Within its churchyard lies another great aviation hero.

With its three pubs, expansive green and parish church, Tylers Green still retains its rural charm despite the ever-increasing spread of the town. St Margaret's Church was built in 1854 by Philip Rose, a successful London solicitor who was the friend of Benjamin Disraeli, and whose family would become mayors of Wycombe.

St Margaret's Church and churchyard, Tylers Green. This was the last resting place of Arthur Whitten Brown.

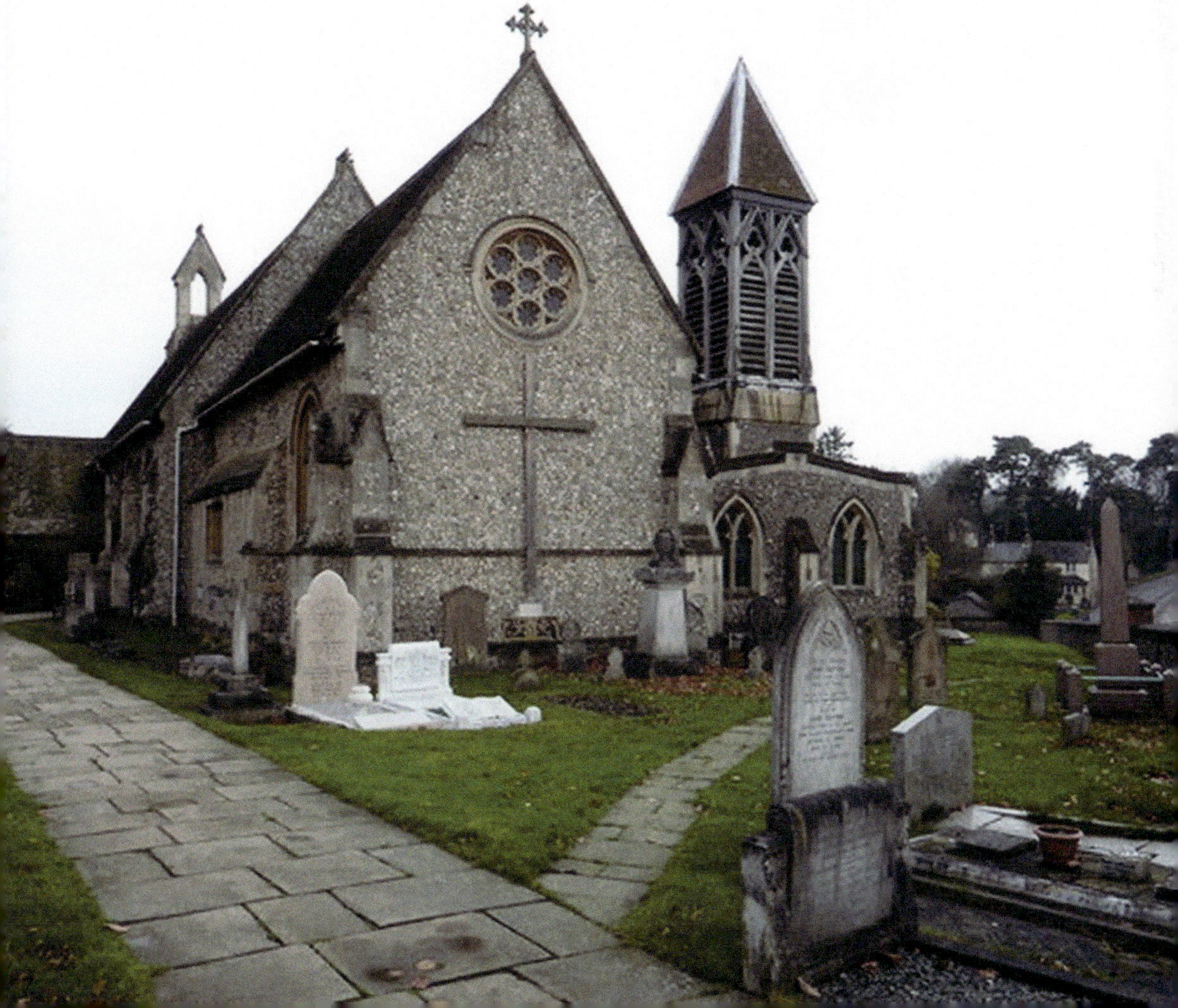

The church is built in the Gothic style, which was popular with the Victorians at the time. In 1891 a bell turret was added, completely constructed of wood. Yet it is in the churchyard where we should stop and contemplate one of its graves.

Arthur Whitten Brown was born in Scotland to American parents. At the outbreak of the First World War he became a Second Lieutenant in 2 Squadron, Royal Flying Corps, as an observer. He was shot down twice over enemy territory and was captured by the Germans and held in a prisoner of war camp.

After the war he began work with the Vickers aircraft company, a consequence of which was that he was asked if he would be navigator on the proposed first transatlantic flight partnering John Alcock, who had been chosen as pilot.

The flight from St Johns, Newfoundland, to Connemara, Ireland, took place on 14 July 1919. It took sixteen hours to complete the 1,980-mile journey, and was the first non-stop crossing of the Atlantic. Alcock and Brown received the Commander of the British Empire from King George V at Windsor Castle and were presented with a prize of £10,000 by Winston Churchill.

Following their great achievement Brown married Margaret Kennedy, a resident of Penn and the daughter of an RAF major. Yet five months later Alcock was tragically killed in a plane crash. Brown went on to serve in the Second World War, but ill health would plague him for the rest of his days. In June 1944 his only son was killed when his plane crashed in Holland.

Alcock and Brown, the first men to fly the Atlantic.

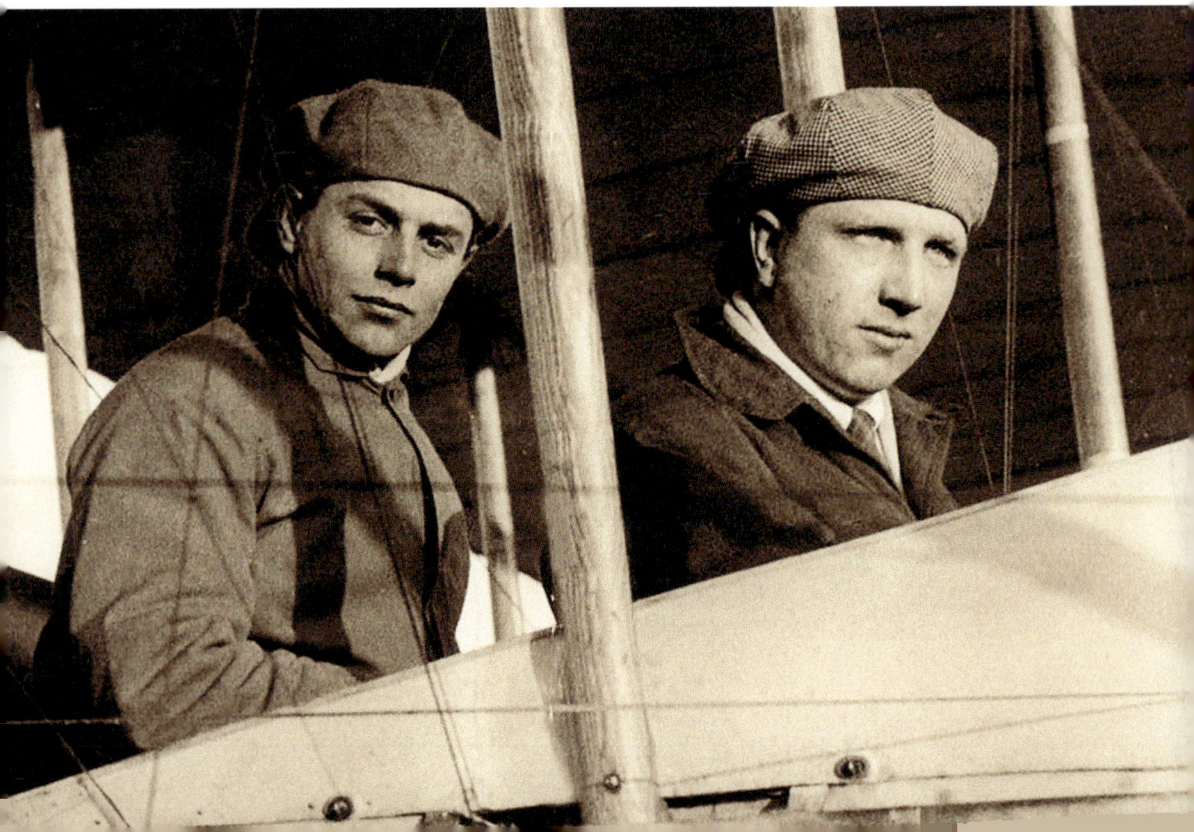

Brown died, aged sixty-two, in October 1948 after an accidental overdose of sleeping pills. He and his wife, who died four years later, are both buried in St Margaret's churchyard.

## 40. St Mary Street

Sometimes two juxtaposed photographs of the same scene taken years apart are at such variance to each other in what they show that one wonders if we are looking at the same location. St Mary Street is no exception. As one entered Wycombe from the south by way of Marlow Hill they would arrive in St Mary Street. As we can see from the photograph taken in 1900, it is an attractive thoroughfare of seventeenth- and eighteenth-century half-timbered buildings. The gates of Wycombe Abbey can be seen on the right and the tower of All Saints Church peeps its head above the roofs and chimney tops.

By comparison the scene today, photographed from approximately the same position as the Victorian picture, is another world altogether. Where the horse and carts and the curious onlookers stand and stare back at us is now the roundabout at the bottom of Marlow Hill.

Part of St Mary Street still runs beyond the present-day fire station, flyover and Legion Hall, and one or two buildings such as the Anchor pub and a Victorian warehouse survive. Ultimately, though, the scene has been once more developed beyond memory.

St Mary Street in Victorian times.

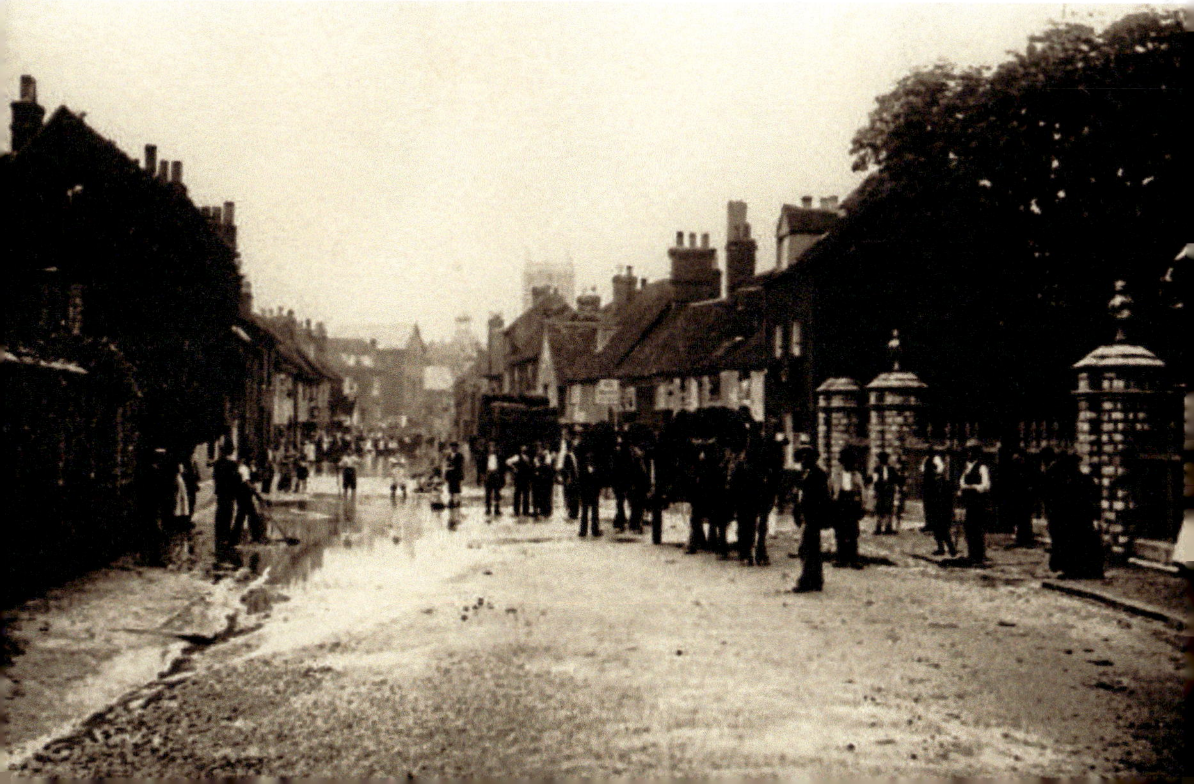

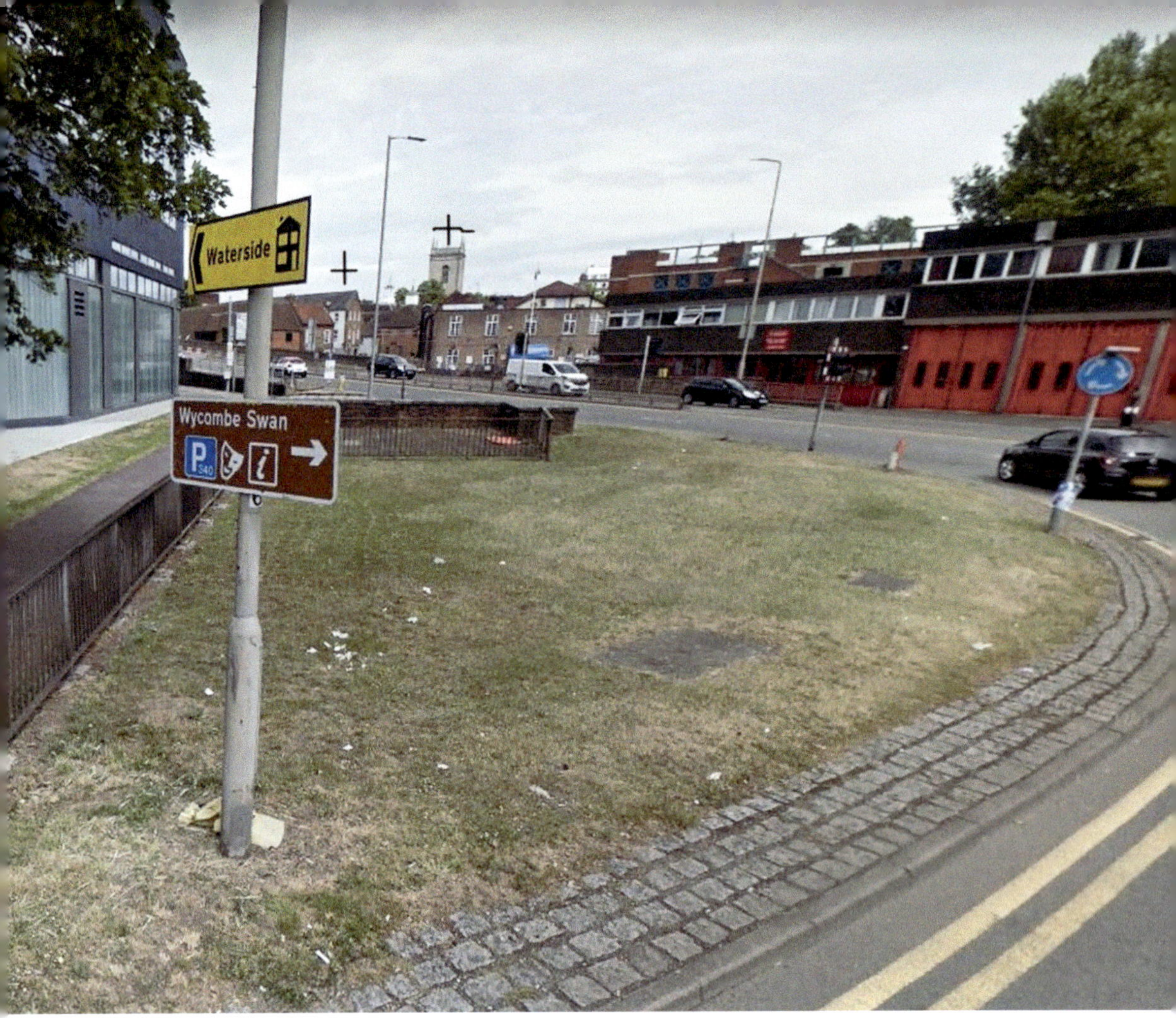


The same location today is unrecognisable.

## 41. Crendon Street

The origins of Crendon Street go way back into Wycombe's ancient history. It was first known as Crendon Lane, an extremely narrow thoroughfare that ran from the high street up past Castle Hill and on to a vanished hamlet called Croyndon or Crendon. The name may have its origin in the dim and distant past and possibly referred to a British chieftain called Creona. The hamlet was once his dwelling place on the hill, or 'don'. Hence Creondon. At the top of the lane near the present railway station was a gate marking the boundary of the borough, which carried on and up its ancient way to Wycombe Heath.

By 1937 Crendon Lane had to be widened to accommodate the increased traffic using the station. Many of the buildings were demolished including the White Lion Inn, Christchurch Sunday school and Dial House, a grand and imposing

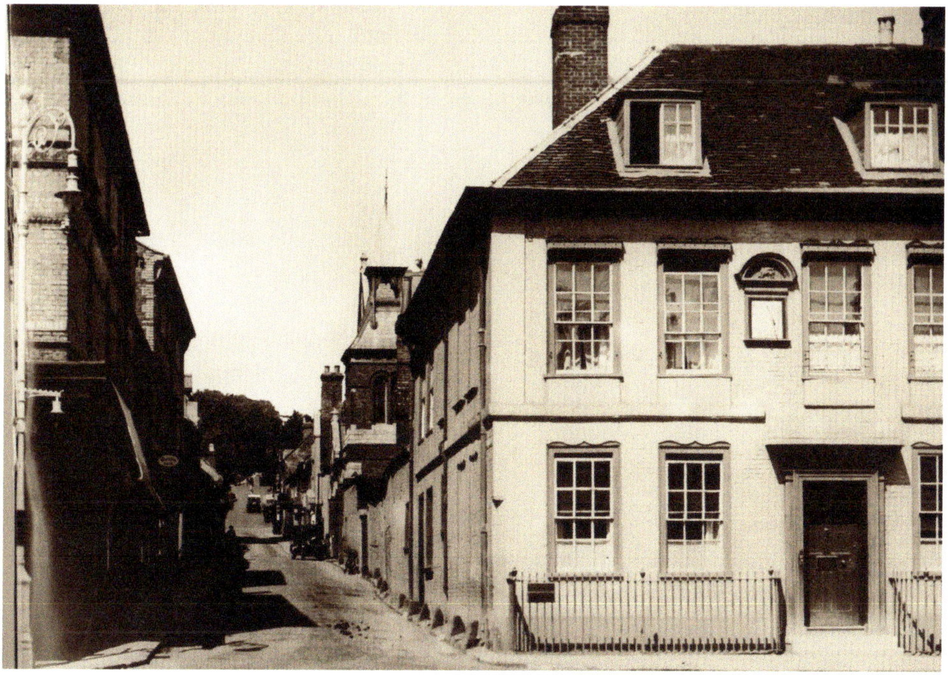

*Above*: Looking up Crendon Street from the high street in the 1930s.

*Below*: Today the scene has changed beyond recognition.

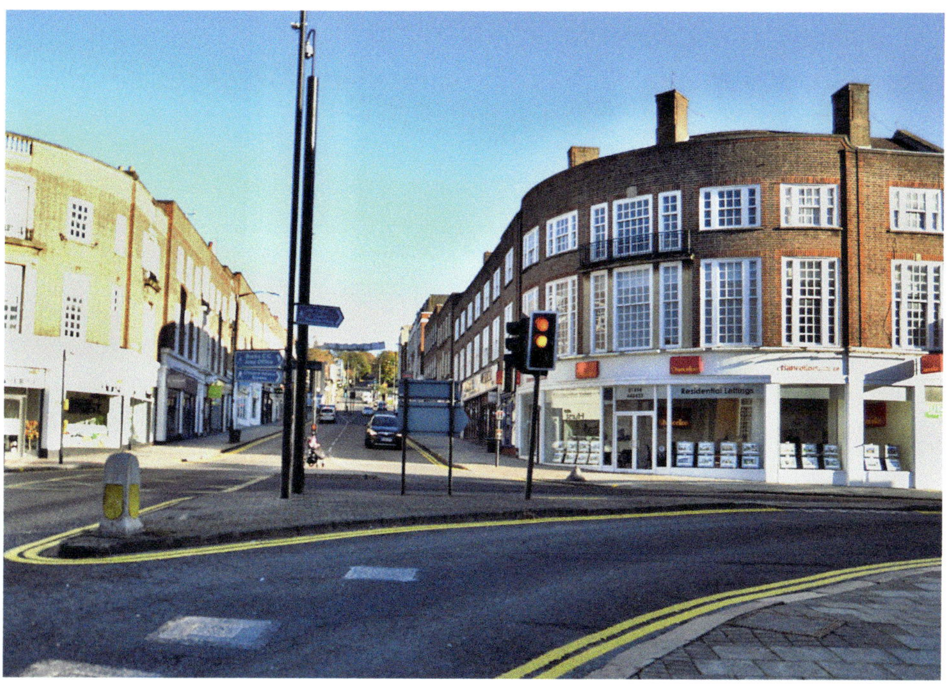

early Victorian mansion. As can be seen in the old photograph, the lane was an attractive thoroughfare containing many old and half-timbered houses. Any newcomer arriving in Wycombe would have been pleased and charmed to enter the town by way of Crendon Lane.

Today, as the modern photograph shows, the scene is totally changed and unrecognisable from the 1930s. Once again the town and its buildings have been sacrificed to the needs of the motor car and our desire to be quickly anywhere else.

## 42. Grand Cinema

The Grand was located on Desborough Road and opened in April 1913. Its first program was a curious choice as it was French film *Zigomar*, the criminal mastermind of French writer Leon Sazles, which had appeared in a French newspaper between 1909 and 1910. An appropriate movie for the Grand as it did indeed have a grand Palladian façade. Reserved seats cost a shilling, while those in the balcony were nine pence. There was also a small stage and dressing rooms for variety acts.

It seems to have been a successful cinema for the next forty years, but was closed for several months in 1953. It was refurbished and reopened soon after.

The site of the Grand cinema on Desborough Road today.

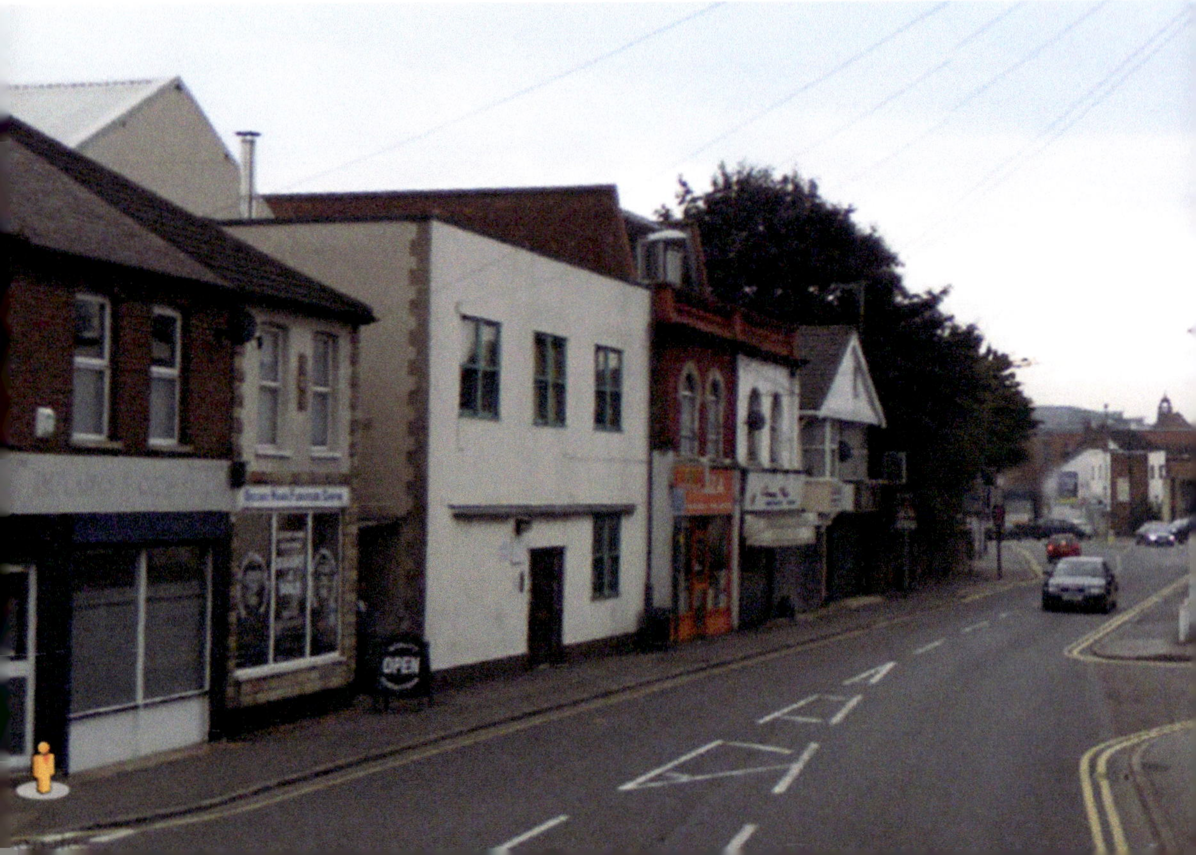

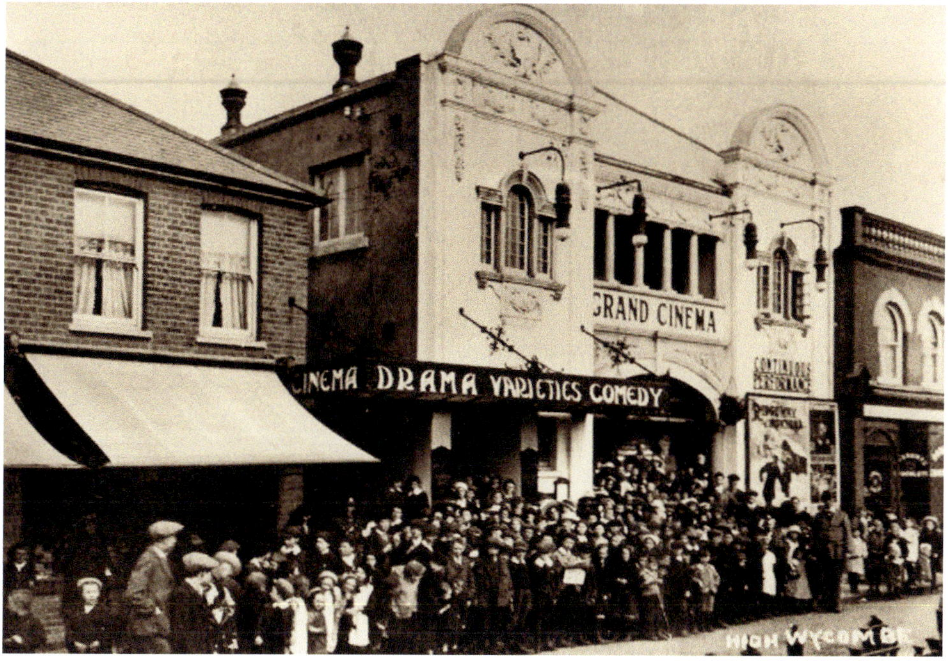


The Grand in its heyday.

However, its days were numbered as it closed for good in September 1962. Part of the building was demolished and the remainder converted into a tailors. Following on from this it once again changed hands and became a furniture showroom for James Blundell, who had converted many other cinemas across the country to sell their goods. It again changed hands for a final time, becoming an electrical store, before being demolished in 1963.

## 43. Rex Cinema

The Rex cinema began as the Electroscope on 28 February 1912. It was a stylish picture palace with a façade with niches that contained statues. It could seat 750 people in its stalls and circle, yet, curiously, it was closed, without reason, in 1930. After standing derelict for some months, it reopened as a remodelled small deluxe cinema with a reduced seating capacity. In December 1937 it was renamed the Rex and opened with Claudet Colbert in *I Met Him in Paris*.

Interestingly, the remodelling design in the art deco style was by Kenneth Freise Green. He was the son of William Freise Green, one of the fathers of early cinema and the inventor of the motion picture camera. The Green family was important in the history of British cinema as Claude Green, Kenneth's brother, founded Elstree Studios.

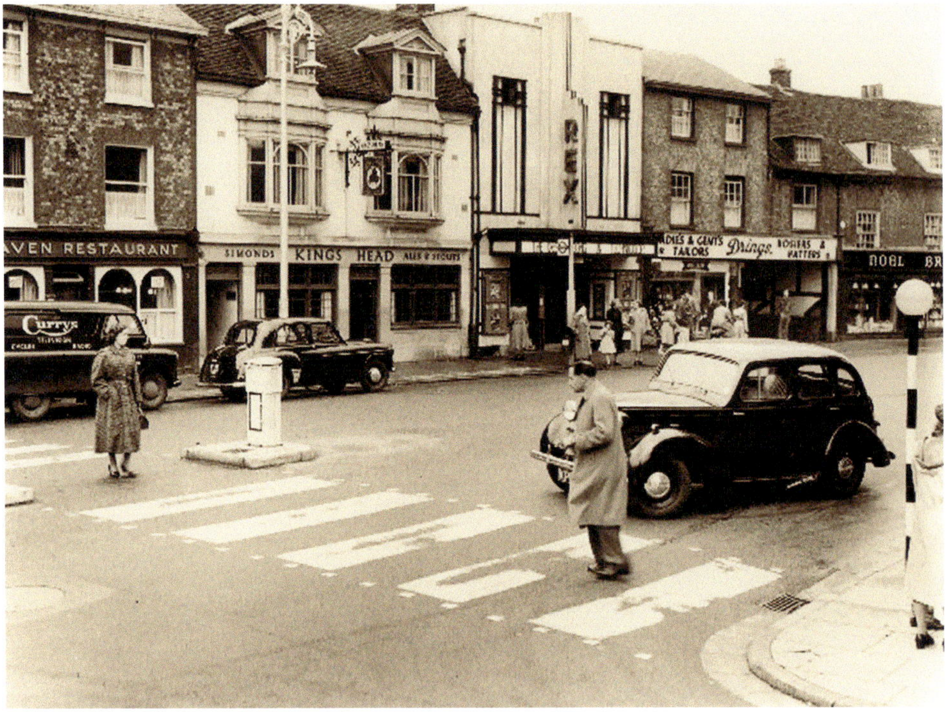


*Above*: The Rex cinema on Oxford Road in the 1950s.

*Below*: The same location today.

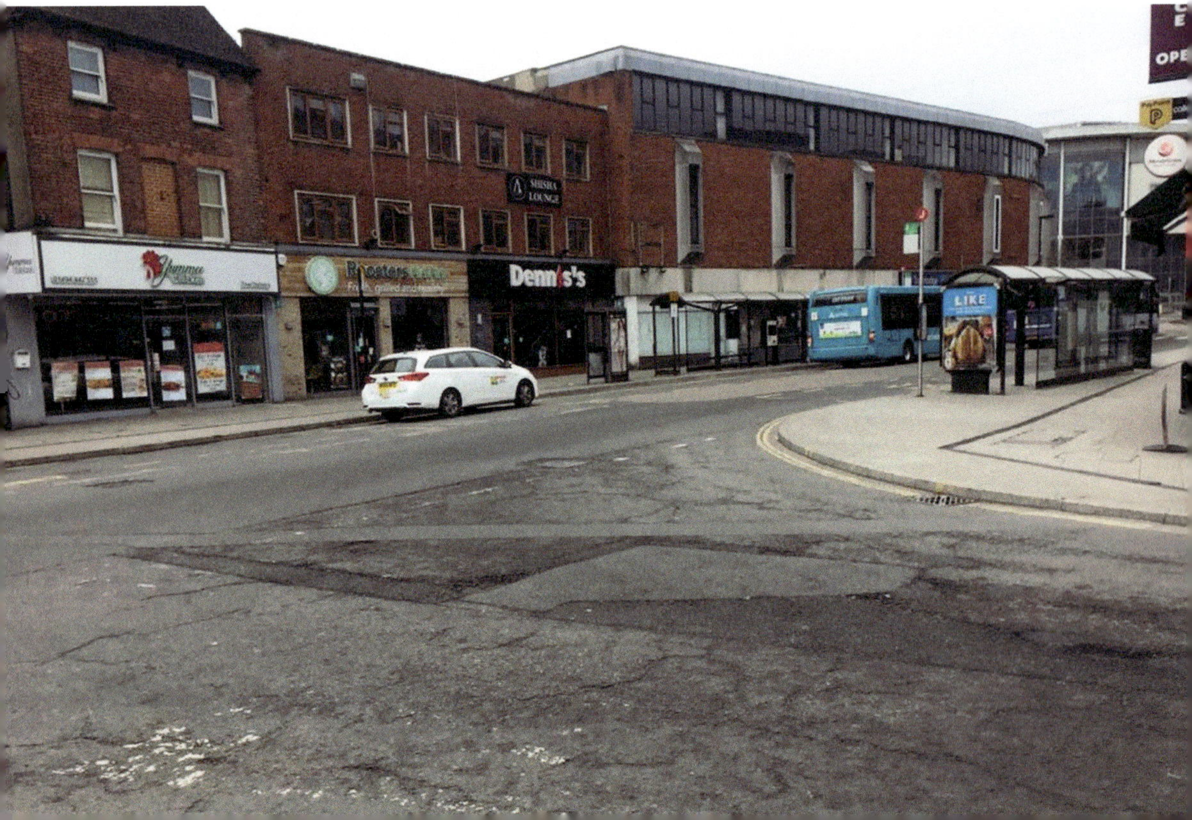

In April 1941, British crooner/singer Al Bowlly made his final performance at the Rex. Bowlly was offered the chance to stay in Wycombe, but chose to catch the last train back to London. That night he was killed in a German bombing raid.

Sadly the Rex closed its doors on the 30 January 1965 with a program of Yul Brynner in *Flight from Ashiya* and Stewart Granger in *The Secret Invasion*. The picture palace went the way of many cinemas across Britain and fell victim to the power of television. It hung for another four years before being demolished in 1969. Today the site is occupied by retail outlets.

## 44. Palace Cinema

Modern-day High Wycombe seems to have become a town of estate agents, shopping centres and fast-food outlets. Yet, in the not too distant past, many townsfolk sought their pleasure either in the public houses, which Wycombe once thrived in, or the cinema. There were at least four, and it was possible to view a different movie every night throughout the week.

Today the town is served by two vast modern cinema complexes showing the latest blockbuster movies in high definition and pristine sound. Back in the 1950s and 1960s, however, people were prepared to queue in line at the cinema to watch films that seem, today, to crop up regularly on daytime television. One of the town's most popular cinemas was the Palace, situated on Frogmore.

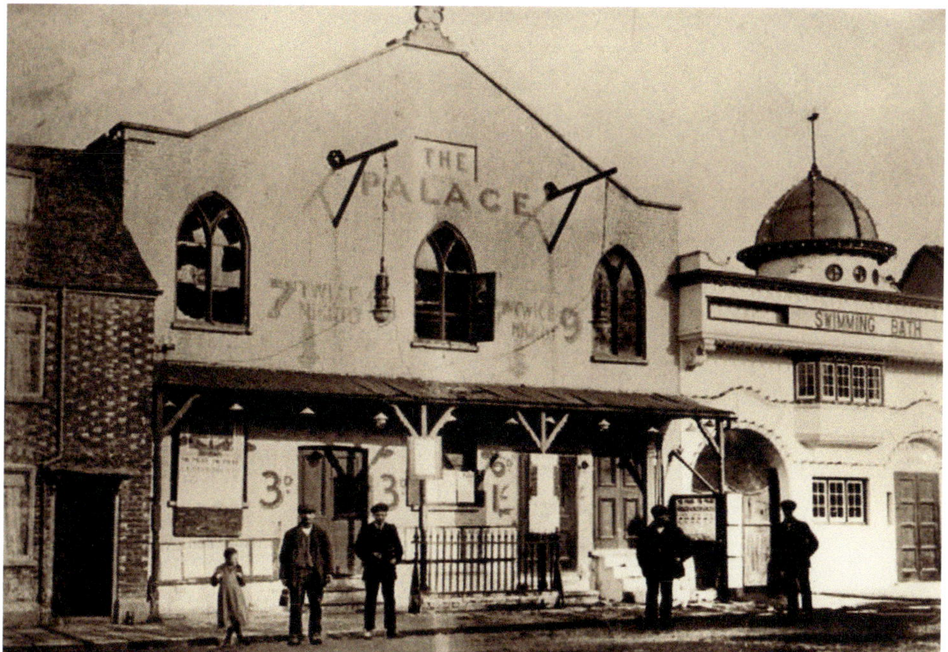


The Palace cinema on Frogmore in its early days.

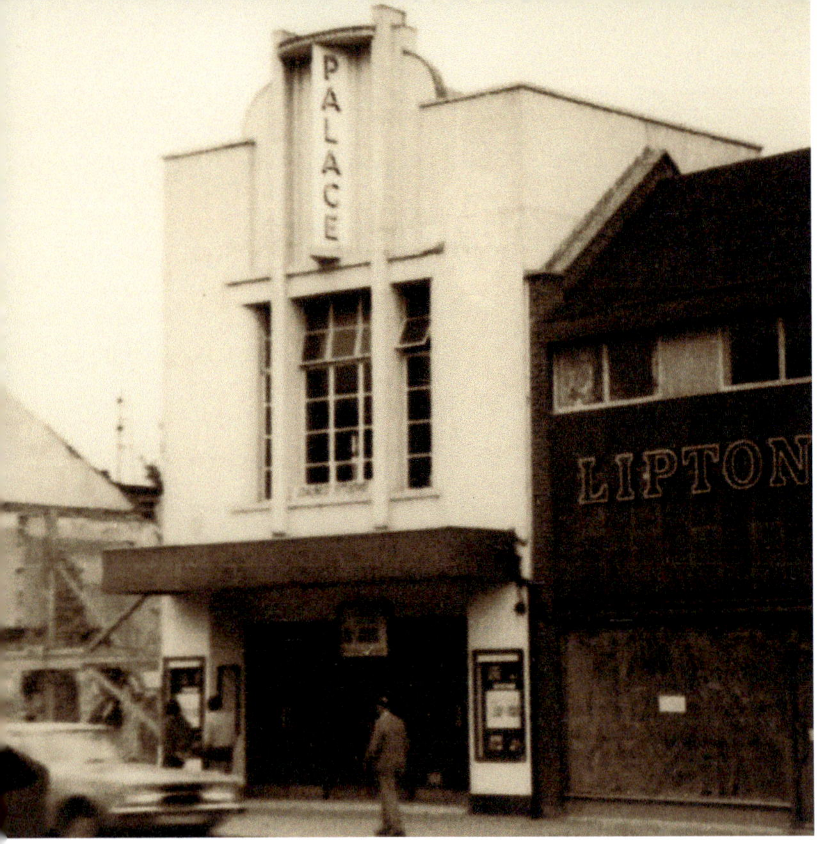


*Left*: The refronted Palace in the 1970s.

*Below*: The site today has become the entrance to the Chilterns Shopping Centre.

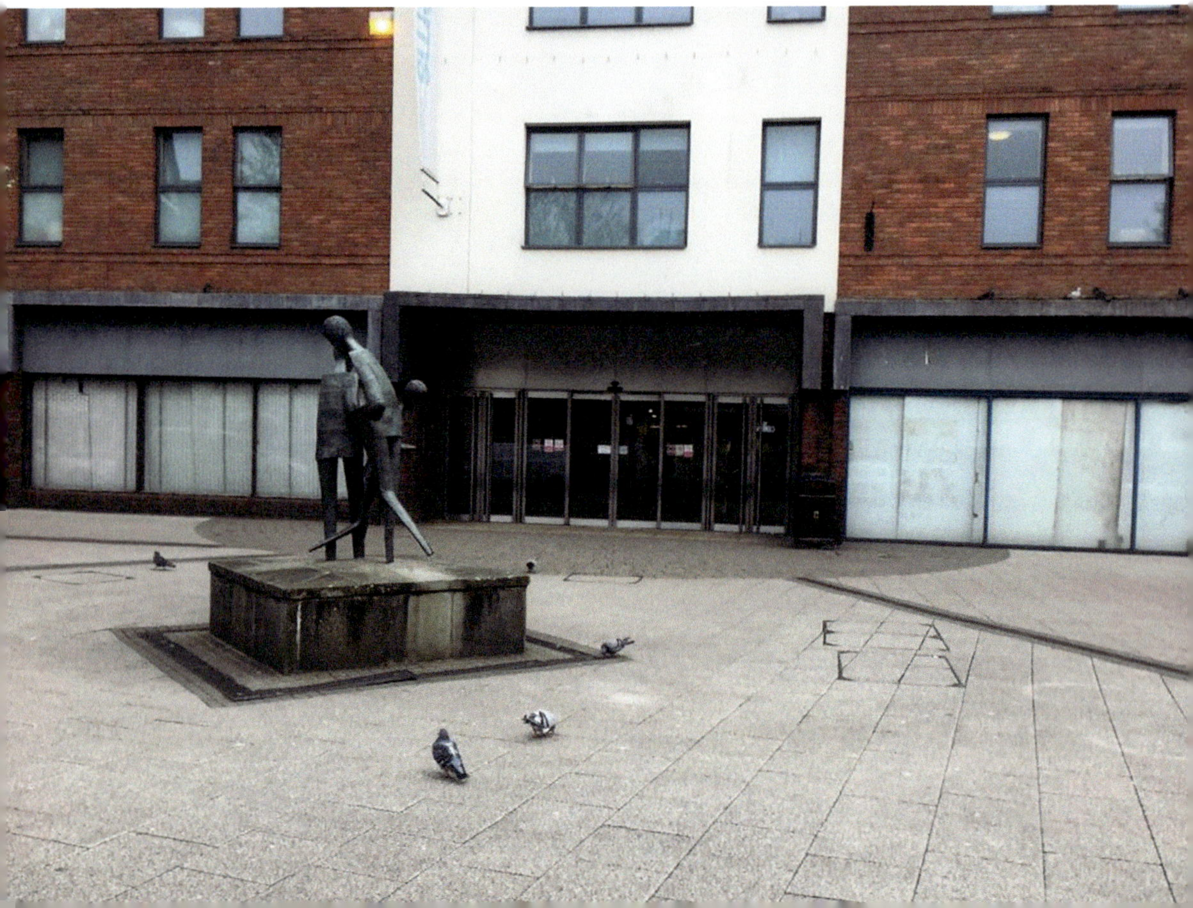

It was designed by Gilbert Booth and opened on 2 December 1922. Its frontage was a mock-Tudor façade with a wood-panelled foyer. The auditorium was designed in the Renaissance style with seating for over 1,200 people. Indeed, it was the biggest cinema in Wycombe. In 1936 it was enlarged to accommodate an extra 400 patrons and given an art deco style modernisation, which included a 40-feet-wide proscenium, a café and a dance hall.

Sadly the Palace closed suddenly in September 1983, with *Psycho II* on the bill. Unaware would-be patrons continued to turn up in the following days only to find the cinema shuttered up, yet still advertising forthcoming movies. The Palace had been made obsolete by the newly opened Wycombe Six complex in Cressex. The cinema was demolished and today the site is occupied by the entrance to the Chilterns Shopping Centre.

## 45. Odeon Cinema

If the Palace had a rival theatre in Wycombe it was the Odeon on Castle Street. It opened as the Majestic Theatre in January 1930, and was the third in a small independent circuit of five Majestic Theatres that opened in the outer London suburbs and south-east England.

It was designed by architect S. B. Pritlove, with a Venetian atmospheric style interior designed by W. E. Greenwood (who was also a director of the

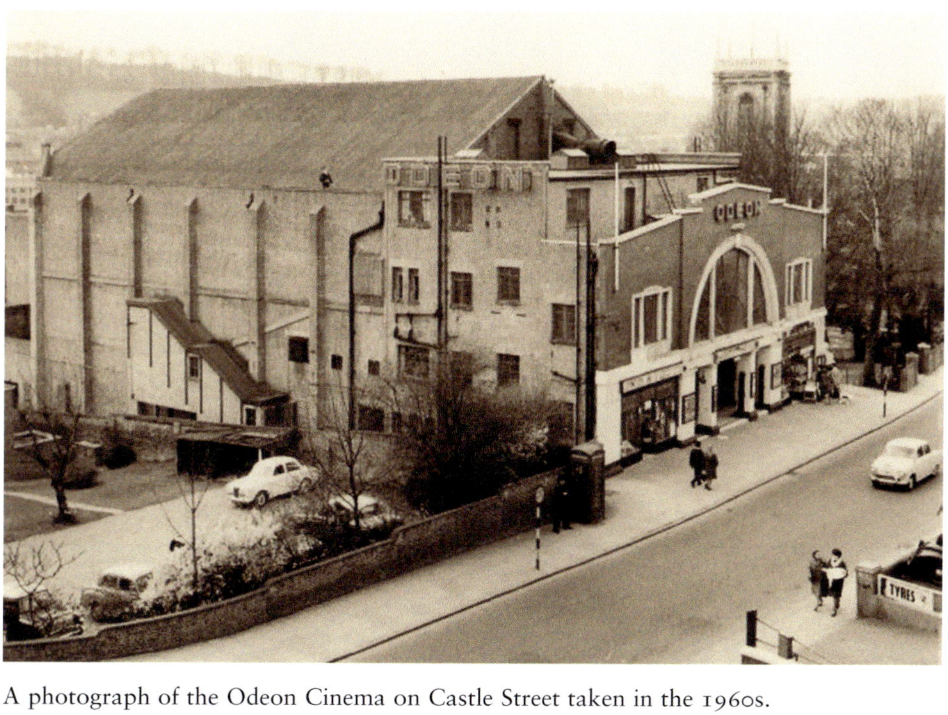


A photograph of the Odeon Cinema on Castle Street taken in the 1960s.

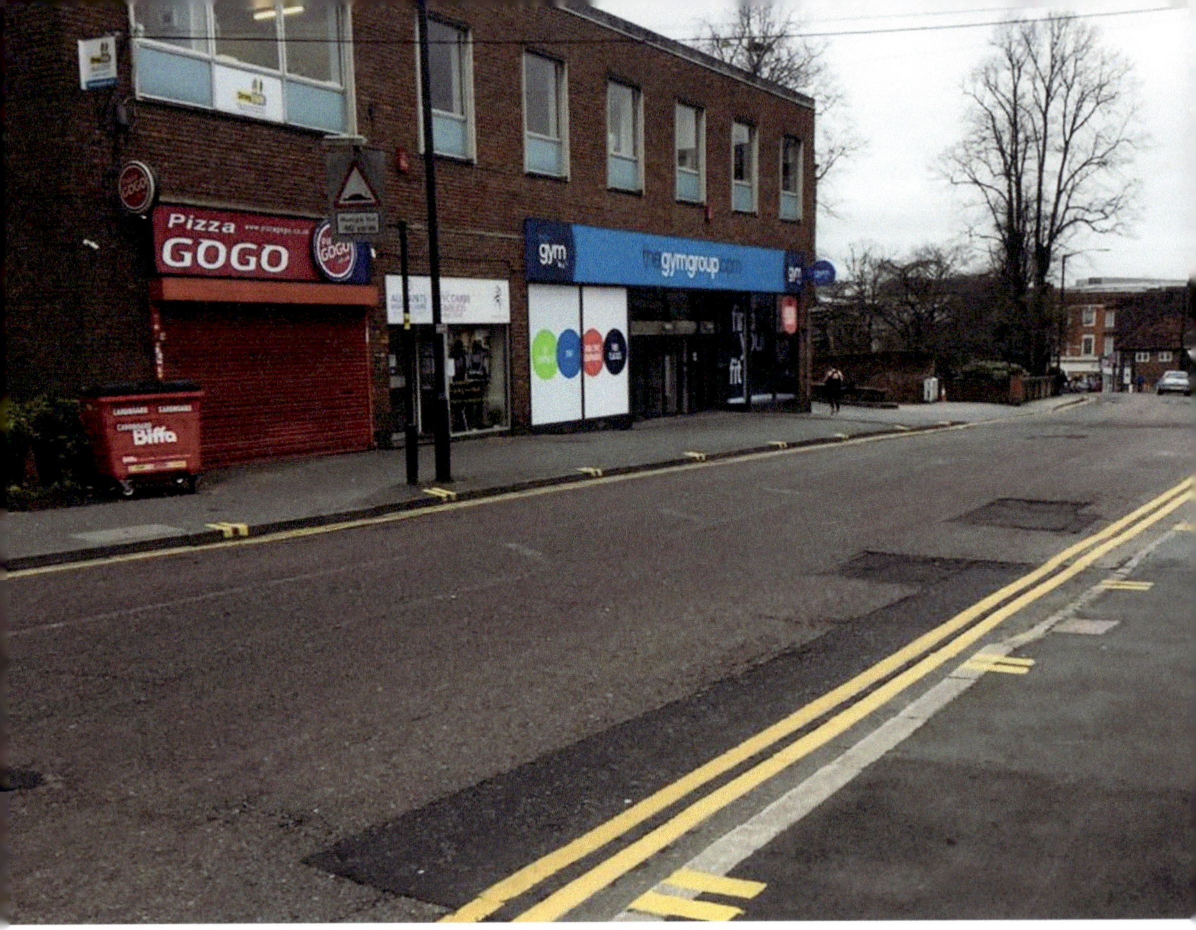


The location today.

operating company). The original seating capacity was for 1,480 and the cinema was equipped with a Compton 2 manual 5 rank organ and had a café and free car park. It was taken over in 1932 by County Cinemas, who were themselves taken over in September 1939 by Oscar Deutsch's Odeon Theatres chain.

It was renamed Odeon from 7 August 1944 and continued until it closed on 25 January 1969 with the unlikely double bill of *Carry On Up The Khyber* and *King Kong Escapes*. Like the Palace cinema, the Odeon was immediately demolished and a Woolworths store built on the site. However, its Compton organ survived and was transferred to Quarrendon County Secondary School in Aylesbury.

## 46. Loakes Park

Wycombe Wanderers Football Club was established in 1884 when a group of workers employed in the furniture trade decided to play friendly matches probably against other factory workers in Wycombe. Originally the team was known as North Town Wanderers, but a meeting in the Steam Engine public house in Station Road in 1887 saw the formation of Wycombe Wanderers FC. In 1895 the club moved to the ground that would become its home for the next ninety-five years: Loakes Park. The following year it joined the Second Division of the Southern League, but would remain an amateur side until 1974.

The Wanderers' first ground was at Spring Meadow, near Wycombe Marsh. When it was sold, an approach was made to Lord Carrington, owner of the estate that included Loakes Park, for permission to hold matches there, with the first game being played in September 1885. The ground was famous for its sloping pitch, where an 11-foot slope ran down and across from the main stand. Despite the oddity of the pitch, the park was to see some memorable games throughout its history.

In February 1950 a record attendance of nearly 16,000 saw the Wanderers beat St Albans 4-1 in the fourth round of the FA Amateur Cup. Probably the most memorable game was played in January 1975, when Wycombe beat Middlesbrough, who were then at the top of the old football league First Division.

The Wanderers played their final season at Loakes Park in 1989-90. The ground had been sold for redevelopment partly for new housing but also for extra car parking for the nearby Wycombe General Hospital.

The last game played by Wycombe Wanderers at Loakes Park in 1990.

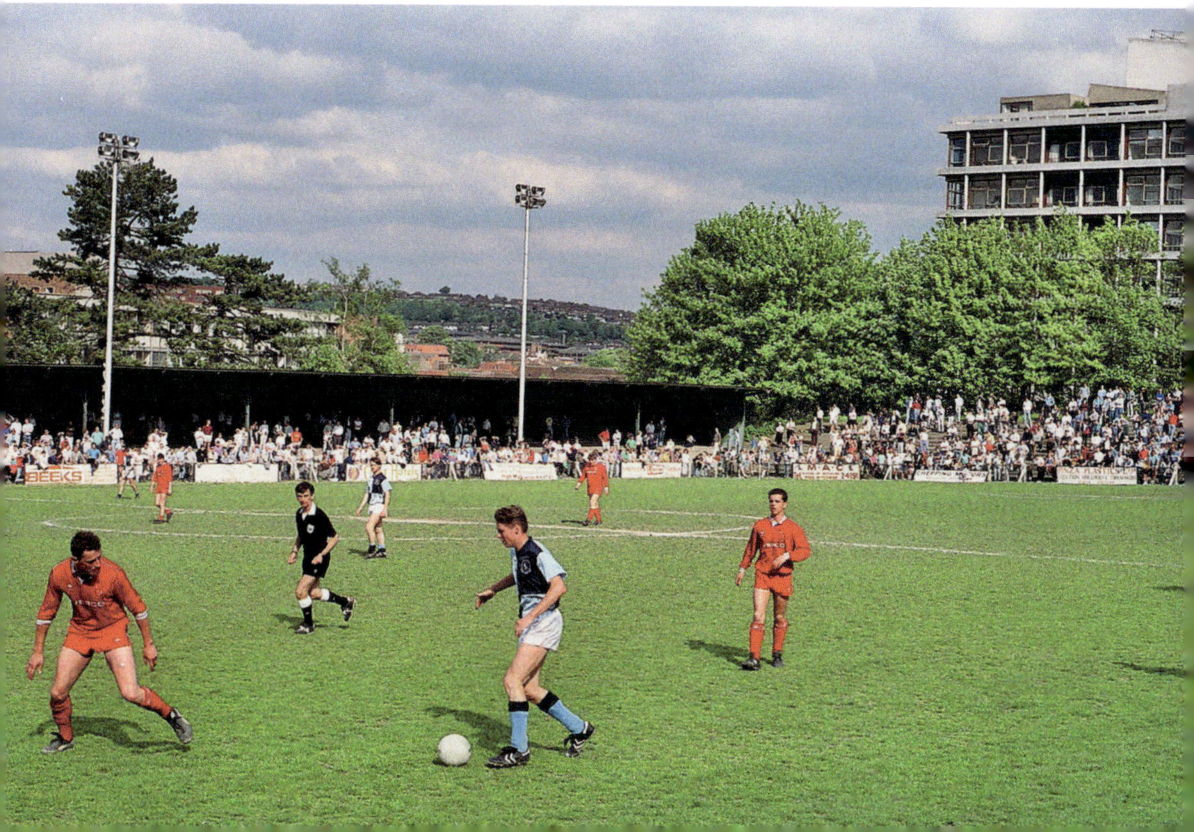

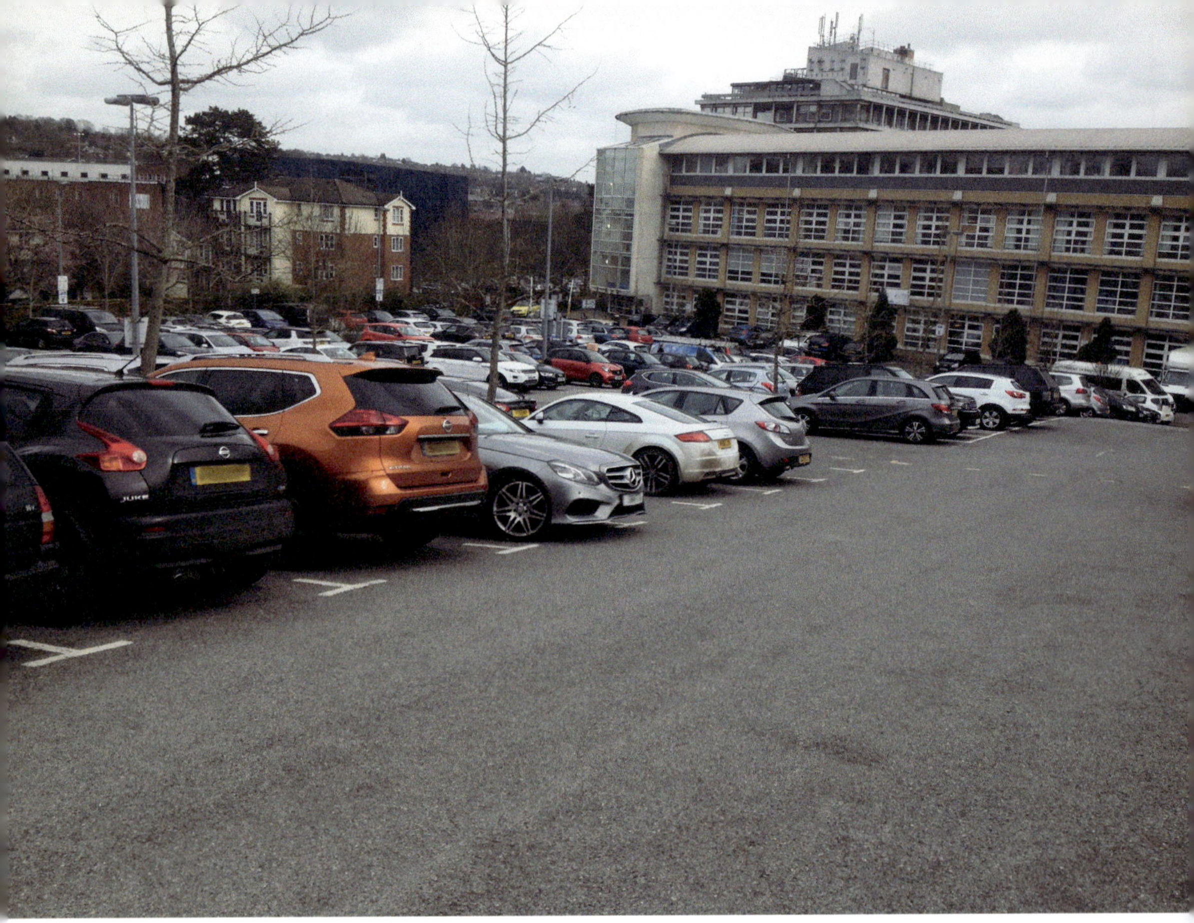

The ground is now the car park of Wycombe General Hospital.

## 47. Loudwater Station

Perhaps nothing demonstrates our distance from the relative past better than the means by which we today travel. Wycombe folk of today think it's nothing to get in their cars and drive 20 miles to another town just to do some shopping. We think it normal to visit friends who live in another county and return within the hour. We take our children every morning lengthy distances on the school run that would make the people of 1950s Wycombe think crazy. We travel today with the soul intention of getting from A to B in the quickest possible time.

Yet there was a time when the prospect of a journey was something to look forward to and be excited about. Where timetables were consulted, departures prepared for, return journey times noted, and the arrival at a train station an almost mini celebration for the adventure to come.

Perhaps I paint too romantic a picture, but travelling through or to and from Wycombe fifty years ago was a big deal, as one of these photographs shows.

Loudwater station was opened in 1854 by the Wycombe Railway, which would later be taken over by Great Western Railway. It was part of the branch line that

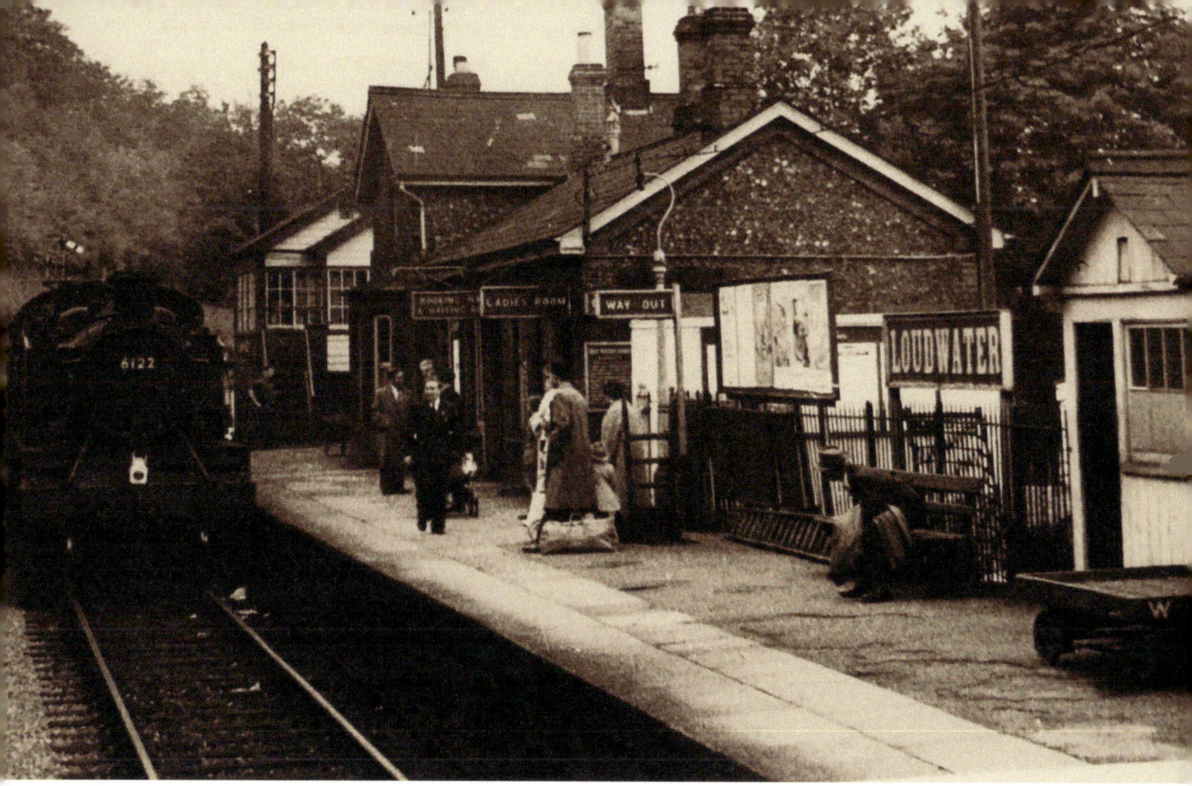


*Above*: Loudwater station in the 1960s when rail travel was still exciting.

*Below*: The station site today.

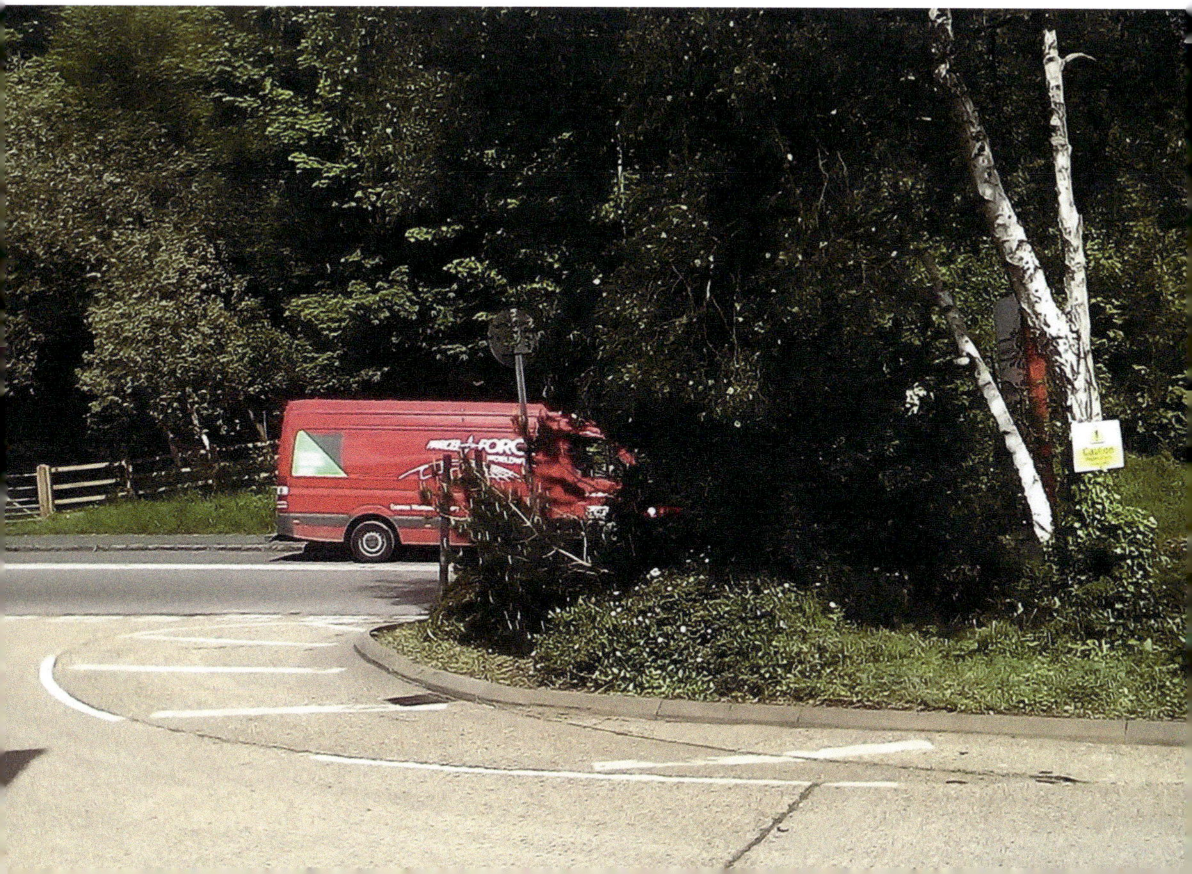

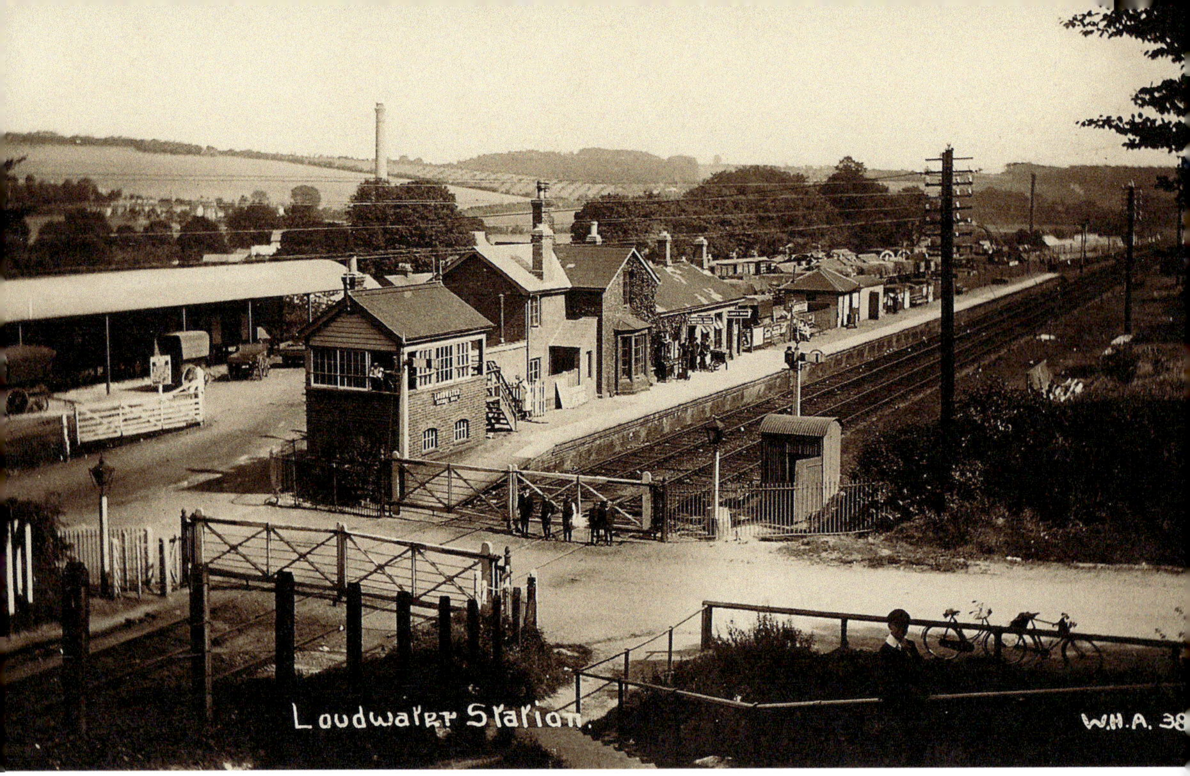


Loudwater station in its heyday.

ran between Wycombe and Maidenhead. Rail travel opened up a whole new world to those who had never ventured beyond the locality of their village or town.

The Victorian photograph shows a station that was all hustle and bustle. There are double tracks, a signal box and a goods yard waiting to transport produce and material to the town or surrounding area. There's also a siding that delivered coal. There are numerous buildings along a lengthy platform, and there is a sense that the railway is the most important place in the village.

The modern photograph of the site of Loudwater station tells another story. The station was closed and demolished in 1970, and the area replaced with industrial units. Now it has become an almost sterile landscape of modern necessity. Why do we need railways when we can sit in traffic jams all day? Happily, part of the old trackbed still survives and has become a peaceful walk and nature trail.

## 48. Oxford Road

Two juxtaposed pictures that demonstrate how much Wycombe has changed within the last fifty years. The black and white photograph shows Oxford Road in March 1965. The River Wye looks more like a storm drain and is in the process of being culverted. On the left there are a few houses that probably dated back to the late eighteenth or early nineteenth century. Many readers of this book will recognise the premises that would later become Scorpion Records, the best second-hand record shop in Wycombe. On the right is the Free Methodist Church.

Now compare the sixties scene with the same spot today. The view is unrecognisable. On the left the mammoth edifice of Sainsbury's superstore rises up. On the right is the corner of Marks and Spencer's store and the Cineworld cinema complex, with one of the entrances to the bus station. It is indeed another world away, and one which reveals Wycombe to newcomers, not as a market town, but a supermarket town.

Oxford Road in the 1960s.

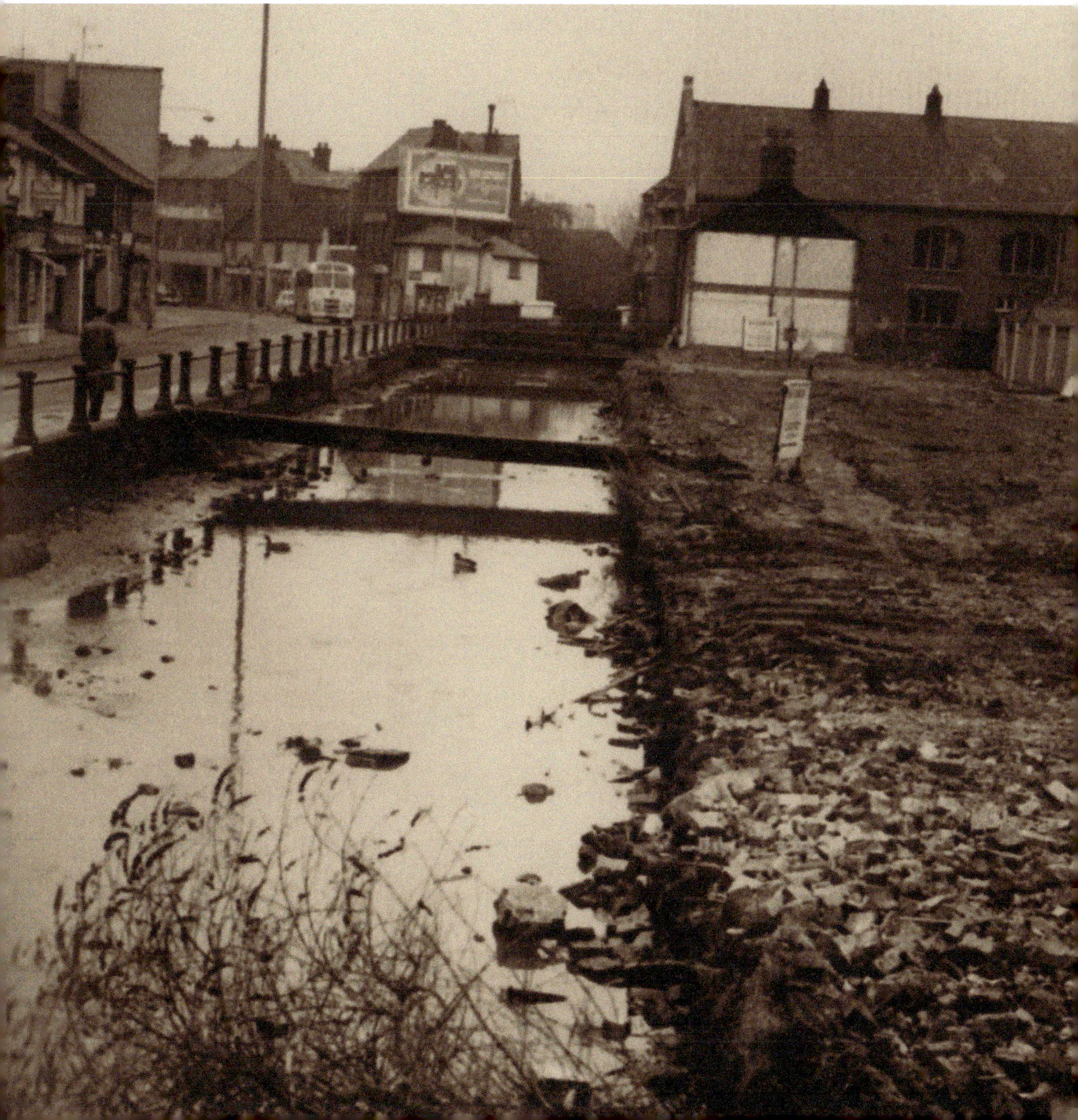

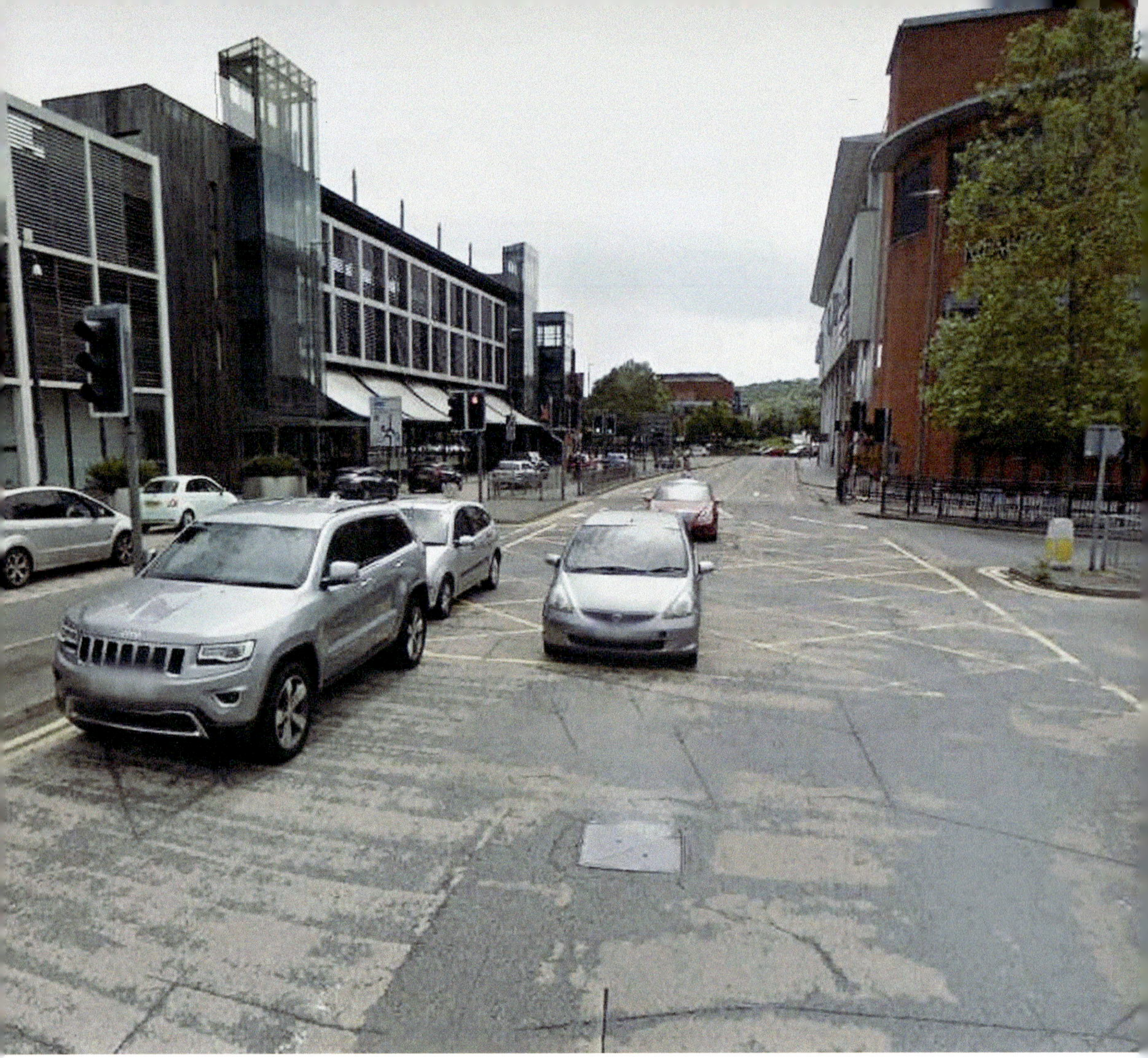

The same location today.

## 49. Wycombe Marsh Paper Mill

Two juxtaposed photographs show how Wycombe has changed in living memory. The black and white picture is of Wycombe Marsh Paper Mills on the London road in the early 1930s. There had been a mill on this site since medieval times, mainly grinding corn. In the Victorian era it was converted to paper manufacture and would come to employ over 200 people.

In 1937 it became Wycombe Marsh Paper Mill and continued in business until it sadly closed in 1994. Up until the 1990s the scene had barely changed from the 1930s; indeed on the right of the picture the pub and the billboards on the corner of Micklefield Road are still recognisable today. By contrast the left of the photograph is another story.

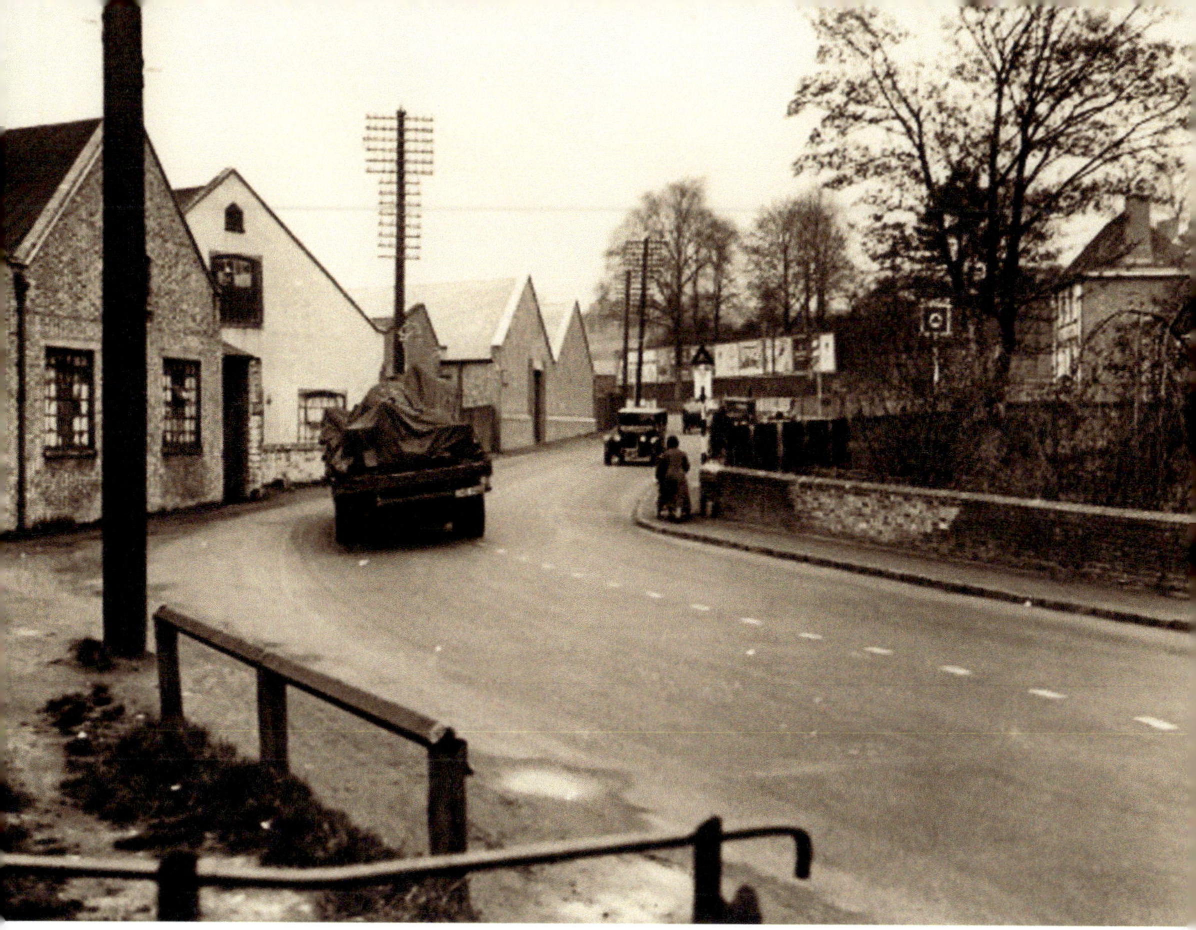

*Above*: Wycombe Marsh Paper Mill on London Road in the 1930s.

*Below*: The same location today is another world away.

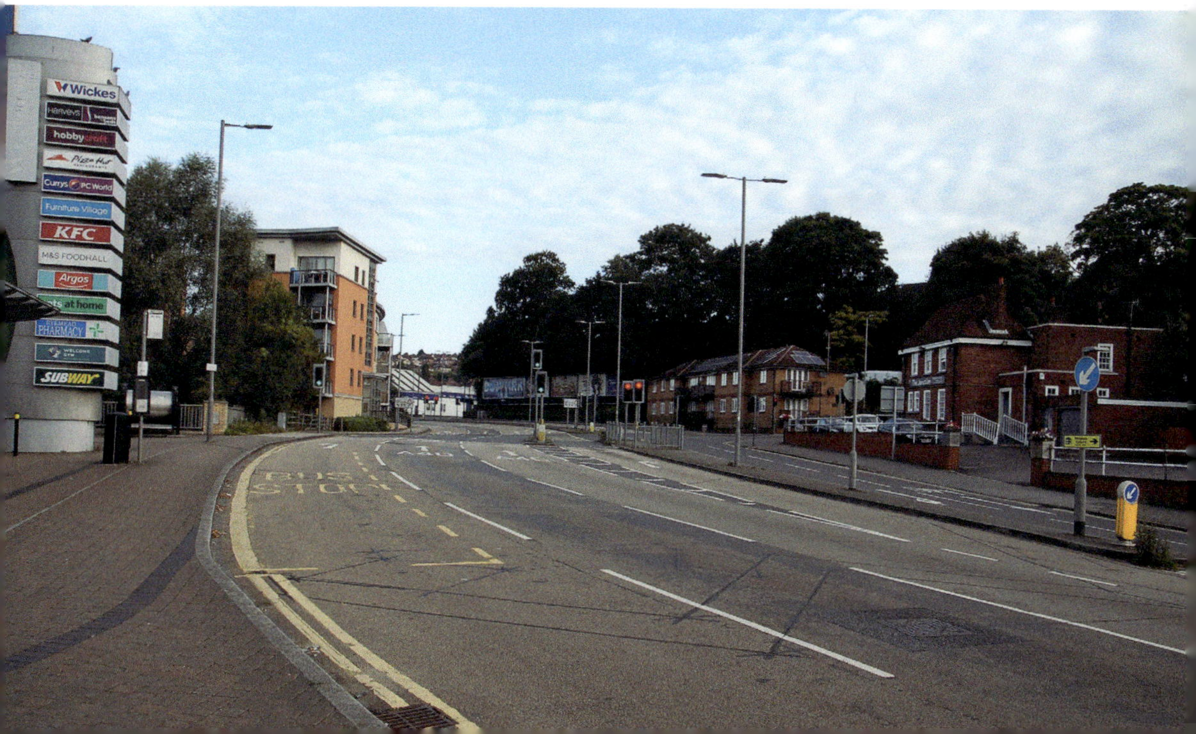

The site is now occupied by the Wycombe Marsh Retail Park, which contains thirteen stores, takeaway outlets and substantial parking. Who needs paper or corn when you can shop until your heart's content?

## 50. Priory Road/Church Street

The ever-changing nature of Wycombe's buildings and landscape is thought to be a modern phenomenon, and the product of a need to constantly reinvent itself and stay ahead of developments and improvements in neighbouring towns. As always, nothing is new as these three pictures demonstrate.

They are of the corner of Priory Road and Church Street. The first is from 1895 and show a pleasant grouping of buildings including Turner wholesale and retail stationers on the right. Next to it is J. N. Hills refreshment rooms. It has a delightful Dickensian shopfront, and one expects one of Dickens colourful characters to emerge into the sunshine. Adjacent to the rooms is the furniture warehouse of E. P. White. All are probably half timbered in construction with later Georgian and Victorian façades, possibly dating back to the seventeenth century.

Ten years later and the scene has changed with the furniture warehouse demolished and replaced with Mcilroys and Turner's store. This building would later form part of the Marks and Spencer's store.

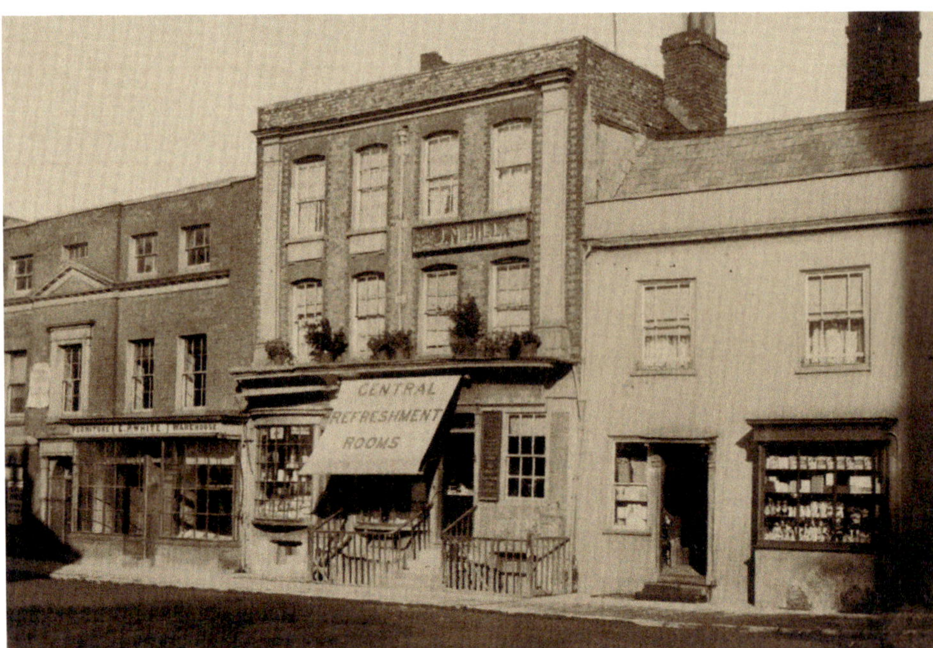


The corner of Priory Road and Church Street in 1895.

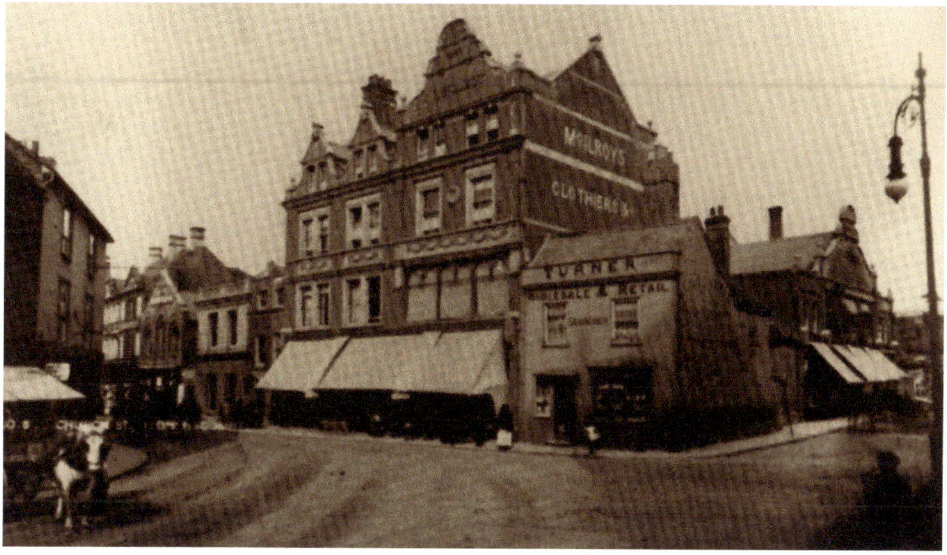


*Above*: The same location ten years later.

*Below*: The same scene today.

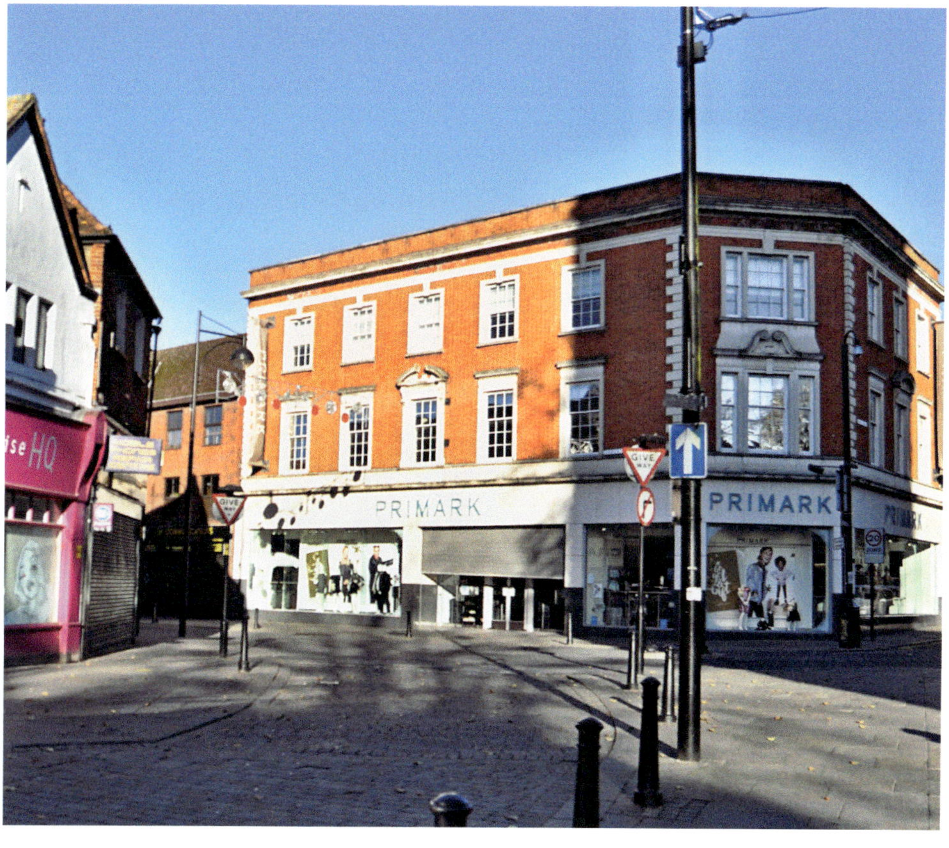

# Acknowledgements

I would like to thank all those who helped during the writing of this book: Jackie Kaye, the Wycombe Historical Society and Mick Silverthorne. Thanks also to the many people who allowed me to use their photographs. Special thanks to all those at St Mungos Centre including Dennis, Ralph, Morris, Stuart Shetake, Stacy Tonbridge and Mrs Johnson. As always thanks to my wife, Sue, and daughter, Bex, for keeping me sane.

# About the Author

Eddie Brazil was born in Dublin in 1956, and later raised in South East London. He is a writer, photographer and paranormal historian. He is co-author, with Paul Adams and Peter Underwood, of *The Borley Rectory Companion* and *Shadows in the Nave*. In 2012 he wrote *Extreme Hauntings* with Paul Adams and in 2013 published *Haunted High Wycombe*.

He has also written *A Bloody History of Buckinghamshire* and in 2017 wrote *Secret High Wycombe*. In 2018, Eddie published *Camberwell from Old Photographs* and acted as advisor, along with Paul Adams, on the movie *Borley Rectory, the Most Haunted House in England*. He is also a guitarist and in 1983 wrote the theme music to the British comedy film *Expresso Splasho*. He lives with his wife in High Wycombe.